Mind Over Mirror

The Body Image Recovery Book for Women

Paetyn Alexander

Little AP Publishing

Contents

Introduction

Let me tell you a story. In sixth grade, our class went on a ski trip. Little did I know that this seemingly innocent outing would mark the beginning of my lifelong battle with body image. Picture this: I was standing in line with my classmates to rent skis, excitement filling the air. Then, our teacher announced that he'd have to weigh each of us — in front of the entire class!

When it was my turn to step onto the scale, a sense of unease crept over me. I've always felt quite self-conscious, being the tallest girl in class and all—even towering over some of the boys. The scale read 124 pounds. A knot formed in my stomach.

"Wow, that's a lot!" My teacher's words hung in the air, cutting through me like a knife.

And then came the laughter from my classmates. Everyone found it funny. Everyone was in on the joke... except for me.

That day, I felt the weight of shame settle upon my shoulders. I started believing that I didn't measure up. It would take decades to shake these feelings off, but by then, I was deep into dieting and disordered eating. Still, I never ever did feel like I was "the right size."

In an interview for Buzzfeed, writer and musician Kaelin Tully shared that at only eight years old, she refused to wear jeans for fear that others would see her chubby thighs. At fifteen, she was totally convinced there was something inherently wrong with how she looked. To combat her perceived flaws, Kaelin turned to extreme measures. She counted calories meticulously and spent hours on the treadmill, hoping to be "the right size." As the pounds began to drop, she felt a fleeting sense of victory, but it was only external. Beneath the surface, Kaelin still couldn't stop comparing herself to others and constantly picking out her so-called "problem" areas. No matter what the numbers said, her arms never stopped feeling too chubby, her butt too flat, her stomach not toned enough. Even her legs, strong from years of horseback riding, filled her with shame and felt all wrong (Guillaume, 2015).

My story and Kaelin's are unfortunately only two out of millions. Issues surrounding body image affect so many people—women, especially. Reports show that up to 91% of women express dissatisfaction with their bodies. What's even more concerning is that many of us resort to extreme measures in pursuit of "the perfect body" when the truth is that only 5% of women naturally have the body type that's often portrayed as the ideal in American media (DoSomething.org, n.d.). Talk about setting ourselves up for disappointment!

But it's never really just how we look, is it? It's about how we feel: the pressure, shame, unworthiness, inadequacy, stress, sadness, frustration, hate, and anger that we impose on ourselves every time we look in the mirror. Knowing that so many women, especially young ones, are experiencing this is precisely why I want to share what I've learned over the years.

I call it the S.P.A.R.K.L.E. framework! Here's how it works:

Start with understanding: Unravel the mysteries behind body image and gain priceless insights to jump-start your journey toward genuine self-acceptance and confidence.

Pave the road to self-compassion: Learn how to practice compassion toward yourself and your body.

Accept body positivity: Dive into the body positivity movement—what it truly is and isn't—and discover how to live your life guided by its principles.

Rewrite the narrative: Utilize simple yet effective strategies for combating body negativity with love.

Know how to care for your body: Empower yourself by giving your body the care it deserves.

Lean on function, not aesthetic: Say goodbye to superficial standards and learn to embrace your body's true potential by prioritizing function over appearance.

Establish a body-positive future: Set up actionable steps for a future where self-love and acceptance reign supreme.

With this simple yet powerful framework, you'll befriend your mind and body quicker than I did. Are you tired of scowling at your reflection every time you face the mirror? Then it's time for a change!

Step into a brighter future, brimming with love and positivity for the vessel that's faithfully carried you through life's ups and downs: your body.

Start with Understanding

*F**eeling beautiful has nothing to do with what you look like, I promise.* -Emma Watson

In a post for Brave Heart Wellbeing, Michelle Daw opened up and shared her experience. When she was eight years old, as she stepped on a scale, she vividly remembers her dad commenting that she weighed too much for her age. Since then, she felt different from her peers. It didn't help her growing insecurities that she attended an all-girls boarding school where she constantly received comments like "Will you ever lose weight?"

Despite not being bullied, Michelle often felt judged by others. She couldn't bring herself to shop at the same stores or wear the latest fashions because she believed she was "fat" and "ugly." As an adult, Michelle admitted that she continues to confront these feelings.

"Sometimes, I feel like my eight year old self, hurt by words and feeling judged by others," she wrote (Daw, 2021, para. 5).

Michelle's story highlights an issue that affects many women: body image. But what exactly is it?

The Stepping Stones of Body Image

Body image refers to the perception, thoughts, and feelings you hold about your own body, including its size, shape, and unique attributes. It is frequently mistaken for self-esteem, which is a related but distinct concept. Self-esteem extends beyond physical appearance to encompass broader feelings of self-worth, including skills, qualities, achievements, and relationships. Body image, however, remains focused on your looks.

A negative body image involves feeling unhappy or uncomfortable with your physical appearance. This can manifest in various ways, whether consciously or unconsciously. You might find yourself avoiding buying new clothes or looking into mirrors, refusing to wear certain clothing items like crop tops, or hiding parts of your body you believe are flawed. All this hiding and avoiding sends a message to your subconscious that your body is wrong, bad, or undesirable.

Additionally, you might constantly criticize your body, telling yourself it needs to be something different—maybe taller or stronger—to be considered attractive. You might wish for different physical features, like straight hair or a leaner body type, and compare yourself to unrealistic standards of beauty. In extreme cases, you might even engage in abusive behaviors toward yourself, such as negative self-talk, starvation, or excessive exercise (Johnson, 2022).

Consider this scenario: As you scroll through social media, you can't help but compare yourself to the seemingly flawless images flooding your feed. However, you never quite measure up. Instead, you find yourself nitpicking at your own perceived flaws even more, leading to feelings of dissatisfaction, self-consciousness, and insecurity. After an hour or two of scrolling, liking pictures, and saving #bodygoals posts, you're left feeling bad about yourself. Has this ever happened to you? This is what struggling with negative body image may look like.

On the other hand, having a positive body image involves embracing and loving your body just as it is. This means that even if you feel dissatisfied with certain parts of your body, you still respect and accept them. For example, you're at the beach with friends, enjoying the warmth of the sun and the sound of the waves. As you walk along the shore, you notice people of all shapes and sizes. Instead of comparing yourself to them or feeling self-conscious, you are focused on the joy of being present in the moment. This is what is possible with a healthy body image!

A positive body image allows you to maintain a balance between acknowledging areas for improvement while also appreciating the unique qualities that make you who you are.

How Does Body Image Form?

The formation of body image, whether positive or negative, begins early in life because "young kids and adolescents are very impressionable," according to Paakhi Srivastava, an assistant research professor at the Center for Weight, Eating, and Lifestyle Science at Drexel University in Philadelphia (Lawler, 2022, para. 17).

One major influence is how we absorb societal norms, especially from various types of media exposing us to "perfect" bodies. For example, seeing celebrities with "ideal" figures on TV or social media might make us feel like we need to look like them to be considered attractive or to be accepted by others. When children experience this pressure and perceive themselves as falling short, it often triggers feelings of shame or inadequacy. Surveys reflect this impact, with 25% of young people attributing their body image issues to celebrities and a larger 40% citing social media as a significant factor (Mental Health Foundation, n.d.).

Experiences of appearance-based bullying, whether from peers or family members, also have a significant influence on body image development. Reports show that children in higher weight categories are 63% more likely to be bullied. Meanwhile, one in three children with differences in their appearance, such as scars, marks, or other visible conditions, has received hurtful comments related to it (Anti-Bullying Alliance, n.d.). Even seemingly harmless remarks about a child's size or looks can leave lasting scars well into adulthood, as evidenced by the stories you've read here so far. Conversely, positive influences, such as a supportive family and group of friends, can help mitigate damage to a child's body image.

According to the National Eating Disorders Collaboration (n.d.), there are four components to body image:

Perceptual: This refers to how you view your body, which might not always match reality. For example, you might look in the mirror and believe you are overweight, when in reality your actual weight is within a healthy range. Despite everything being normal, your perception may be distorted, leading to feelings of dissatisfaction.

Affective: This refers to your emotional response toward your body. How does your reflection make you feel?

Cognitive: This involves your thoughts and beliefs about your body, which can sometimes excessively focus on weight and shape. For example, you might constantly believe you are not thin or muscular enough to be accepted by others or considered attractive. These thoughts may lead to an unhealthy preoccupation with dieting, exercise, or comparing yourself to unrealistic standards.

Behavioral: This pertains to the actions and behaviors you engage in as a result of how you feel about your body. For example, you might avoid social situations or activities that involve showing your body, such as going to the beach. You may also engage in extreme dieting or excessive exercise in an attempt to change your body. These actions are a result of poor body image and can impact your overall well-being.

As you can see, body image formation is pretty complex and is shaped by a combination of internal and external factors.

How Body Image Impacts Women

Body image issues do not discriminate; unfortunately, they can impact anyone regardless of gender, race, age, cultural orientation, or economic status. That being said, studies have shown that, in general, men tend to be more satisfied with their bodies and perceive themselves as more attractive and less overweight compared to women. Men also tend to feel better about themselves when they possess desirable body traits, which can boost their self-esteem and body satisfaction. On the contrary, we, women, typically assess our appearance in a more objective manner, which means that having socially desirable traits doesn't necessarily make us feel better about ourselves (Voges et al., 2019). Therefore, body image issues tend to affect women more frequently and profoundly. In fact, one study revealed that only two percent of women worldwide considered themselves to be "beautiful" (Lindner, 2023).

In addition to societal and cultural pressures, we also undergo various body changes throughout our lives, such as during puberty, pregnancy, and menopause. These changes can significantly influence how we perceive our bodies, as we grapple with accepting and adapting to shifts in our appearance. For instance, weight gain during pregnancy is a common concern. Regrettably, the societal messaging many women hear immediately after childbirth isn't centered around rest and recovery but on quickly "bouncing back" to their pre-pregnancy bodies. This is evident in the countless diet and fitness programs aimed at mothers, which are often not even led by experts on postpartum health. While the "dad bod" is celebrated, the bodies of those who actually gave birth rarely enjoy the same level of acceptance (Ruggeri, 2022).

In an article for Self Magazine, personal trainer and fitness writer Tiffany Ayuda talks about how the "bounce back" culture affected her. Three months after giving birth, Tiffany's belly was soft, her arms less muscular, her legs numb, and the dark lines across her stomach from pregnancy remained prominent. As a woman in the fitness industry, Tiffany had always prioritized strength and function over appearance. She never held unrealistic expectations of her body bouncing back quickly after childbirth because she recognized the gradual and unpredictable nature of the postpartum process. However, social media posts showing other moms seemingly regaining their pre-pregnancy bodies within weeks still triggered feelings of anger, grief, and jealousy in her, challenging her once-healthy beliefs about women's bodies.

Tiffany wrote: "Like many other moms, I felt the societal pressure to do exactly what I did before I had a baby—and to do those things just as well or even better. But newly postpartum parents are often not ready—physically and mentally—to dive right into exercise. I certainly wasn't. I didn't want to throw myself into a workout routine; I wanted to sleep well, to eat my meals at the table instead of multitasking with a baby, and to just sit still" (Ayuda, 2021, para. 38).

Despite this self-awareness, Tiffany admitted that she was still deeply affected by these posts.

Aging is another major concern for us. Discussions about signs of aging, coupled with the physical changes linked to menopause, have been noted to heighten anxiety and exacerbate body image struggles. In fact, many older women express feeling disconnected from their bodies because their appearance doesn't match how they feel inside (Mental Health Foundation, n.d.-b).

Indeed, body image concerns affect women of all ages, not just the young. This is evidenced by a study revealing that as many as 88% of women aged 50 and up are dissatisfied with their bodies, with 71% actively trying to lose weight (Fredrek, 2017).

"It is a myth that older people don't care what they look like," says Professor Nichola Rumsey, co-director of the University of the West of England's center for appearance research. "It doesn't wane—many women in their 80s are still anxious about the way their bodies look, which can even affect their treatment in hospital when their health choices are influenced by aesthetics" (Kay, 2012, para. 3, 8).

Sadly, with each life milestone, it can seem as though we're drifting farther and farther from the ideal body we aspire to achieve, perpetually staining our big moments with feelings of not being good enough.

The Influence of History and Culture on Body Image

Historically, a woman's body was crucial for her survival in societies where men held most of the power. How women looked and their size were determined by what men found attractive and suitable for marriage. As a result, women's bodies, appearance, and health were heavily influenced by what society and culture deemed important. Indeed, we can conclude that the ideal body reflected not only societal norms but also the cultural values of the times.

For instance, in Ancient Egypt, the ideal body was described as slender with a high waist and narrow shoulders. Meanwhile, during the Han Dynasty, Chinese culture preferred slim women with small feet. In the West, throughout the 17th and 18th centuries, artists depicted the ideal woman as curvy and plump. In fact, to achieve this ideal, women of that time commonly wore undergarments known as corsets or stays, which were designed to emphasize a woman's curves by cinching her waist (Van Edwards, 2016).

Across various cultures and time periods, what's considered the ideal body kept evolving, pushing us to constantly try to meet these new standards. At some point, we all wonder: *Why?* Why do we endure tight undergarments for the illusion of curves? Why do we obsess over counting calories in pursuit of this elusive ideal shape? Wouldn't we be free of these expectations if we just... well, stopped participating?

In an ideal world, that would be the case. Sadly, in the real world, that's easier said than done. Our notions of beauty are strongly linked with how we perceive health, wealth, power, and overall success. This has been the case since ancient times. For instance, in ancient China, people believed that a woman's body was her source of beauty and, therefore, her power. Her beauty enables her to ascend in society, influence powerful leaders and warriors, and even bring down empires. Similarly, in Victorian England, a woman's body, molded by fashion trends, reflected her social standing and, therefore, affected her marriage prospects and ability to rise in society (Ngo, 2019).

You can see this in action without even having to crack open a history book! Just pick up your phone and scroll through any social media platform. You'll see that women who fit traditional beauty standards usually get more likes and followers than others.

Social Enforcers of Body Image

So, unfortunately, we're at a disadvantage. From the time we were born, society has echoed a clear and unmistakable message: we prioritize beauty above all else. Don't believe me? Let's explore a well-established psychological phenomenon known as "the halo effect."

"The halo effect" refers to our tendency to associate positive qualities, such as intelligence, kindness, or competence, with people we find highly attractive, even if there is no evidence to support these assumptions. This bias influences various aspects of our lives. In fact, economist and author David Hamermesh found that people considered attractive have a higher likelihood of employment, receive better salaries, are more likely to secure loans with favorable terms, and tend to marry partners who hold higher social statuses (Gruys, 2019). Meanwhile, American workers ranked among the bottom of one attractiveness scale earned approximately 10-15% less annually than someone in the top third. That means they are missing out on nearly a quarter-million dollars in earnings over their lifetime (Brooks, 2021).

Interestingly, even in legal proceedings, it has been observed that attractive offenders often receive lighter sentences for their crimes.

Some are even catapulted to unexpected fame! An example is Jeremy Meeks, whose viral mugshot earned him the nickname "hot convict," which led to a modeling contract and a fan following (Putham, 2015). On the flip side, one study revealed that when less attractive criminals committed a moderate misdemeanor, their fines were approximately four times higher.

Moreover, despite the fact that about 40% of the U.S. population are deemed overweight, weight stigma remains prevalent and enduring. Individuals with heavier weights are often stereotyped as lazy or lacking willpower. These biases can lead to negative attitudes toward them, such as social rejection, discrimination, and bullying. Sadly, about 42% of Americans report having experienced being teased or treated unfairly due to their weight. Physicians and coworkers are cited as some of the most common culprits (Abrams, 2022).

Rebecca Puhl, deputy director of the Rudd Center for Food Policy and Obesity at the University of Connecticut, has been studying weight stigma for two decades. She stated that weight bias remains largely unchanged and may even be worsening in some instances. "Contrary to public perceptions, weight stigma does not motivate people to lose weight. Instead, it worsens health and reduces quality of life. The harmful impacts of weight stigma can be real and long-lasting," she writes (Puhl, 2021, para. 9).

Of course, objectively, we know we don't truly need a flat stomach and toned arms to achieve success or happiness. However, as social creatures, we cannot avoid interacting with others, and we cannot succeed entirely on our own in the world. Additionally, it is in our nature to fear rejection and crave approval and belonging from other people. Indeed, it can feel challenging, even disadvantageous, to go against the grain and opt out of a game that everyone seems to be playing.

Repairing the Damage

Though it may seem daunting to break free from the constant scrutiny of our bodies in a culture that is so extremely focused on appearances, it's important to recognize that it's not impossible. In fact, a healthy body image makes life better!

Studies show that women who feel good about their bodies tend to be more confident, take better care of themselves, and have happier relationships. These factors are strongly linked to better emotional well-being and overall happiness in life. Conversely, a negative body image poses several risks, including engaging in unhealthy behaviors such as dieting, restrictive eating, over-exercising, smoking, and substance abuse. It has also been linked to mental and emotional challenges, such as depression, anxiety, loneliness, and low self-esteem (Collins, 2022).

A damaged body image can show up in many ways in your daily life. In fact, why don't we quickly assess the condition of your body image? Simply answer the following questions (Stanborough, 2020):

Do you use negative or harsh language when describing your body?

Do you go to extreme lengths to avoid seeing or acknowledging your body?

Do you experience intense negative emotions when thinking about your body or appearance?

Do you feel the need to wear heavy makeup or hide your body with clothing or accessories when in public?

Do you feel pressured to keep up with grooming practices, such as plucking, shaving, waxing, or laser treatments?

Do you frequently weigh yourself, measure body parts, or spend excessive time examining yourself in the mirror?

Do you engage in behaviors that intentionally harm your skin or body?

Do you feel the need to undergo cosmetic procedures or surgeries in an attempt to change your appearance?

Do you often feel that your body image affects your relationships, work, or daily activities?

If you answered yes to any of these questions, your body image could be damaged. However, it's important to know that this is not permanent, and there are ways to repair it.

Everyone Can Heal

Yes, you read that right. You have the power to heal your relationship with your body regardless of age—it's never too early or too late to begin! To start, here are some major mindset shifts for overcoming negativity and fostering a healthier relationship with your body.

Check Your Own Biases

The journey toward personal growth always begins with self-reflection. So, start by embracing people of all shapes and sizes. Reflect on the lessons from this chapter, particularly on how societal beauty standards have changed a lot throughout history and only continue to do so. Remind yourself that even the most perfect woman of the 17th century would be considered "overweight" today. It might also help to make a list of people you admire who don't fit typical beauty standards. Think about whether their appearance affects how you see them.

Additionally, try to be more mindful of fat-shaming, weight-based discrimination, and stigmatizing language or actions. Take note of comments or jokes about someone's weight and acknowledge them as they are: inappropriate and hurtful. Monitor your own language and avoid remarking negatively about other people's bodies. Educate yourself further on the impact of fatphobia and weight stigma on mental and physical health. Show empathy and support to friends or family who may have faced weight-shaming or weight-based discrimination. Provide them with a safe space to share their experiences and be their ally.

If you feel comfortable, speak up against weight-shaming or weight-based discrimination when you encounter it. You can also initiate discussions with loved ones about the importance of respecting and embracing bodies of all shapes and sizes. As you continue to practice empathy toward others, you'll find it easier to extend that same compassion to yourself over time.

Factor in Genetics

It has long been hammered into our brains that weight is determined by the number of calories you take in versus how many you burn. It's supposed to be simple. But if it were, then everybody would sport the same bodies just by following the equation. In reality, it's not that simple. I bet you can name a person who eats fast food, ice cream, and cake all the time and never seems to gain weight. And you probably also know someone who gains weight easily. That's because genes play a big role here.

The extent of how much genes affect weight can vary from person to person. For some, genes might only account for 25% of their weight struggles, while for others, it could be as high as 80%. According to research, if you've dealt with excess weight for much of your life and have parents or several relatives who are also on the heavier side, genetics could be playing a big factor. Additionally, if diet and exercise haven't helped you lose weight despite your best efforts, your genes might also be why (Harvard Health, 2019).

Many of us have been led to focus solely on environmental factors, which contributes to stigma. It is important to be aware that genes play a significant role in hunger and fullness cues, metabolism, food cravings, fat distribution in the body, and a person's tendency to use eating as a coping mechanism for stress. So, when you find yourself making negative assumptions about someone whose body type differs from the ideal, remind yourself that those assumptions are likely incorrect.

Weight doesn't necessarily reflect a person's health or willpower. By understanding the role of genetics in your body image, you can start to let go of harmful judgments about others and yourself.

Tackle the Underlying Emotion

Feeling bad about your body is often less about how you look and more about how you feel. It's about the thoughts, emotions, and beliefs you carry inside yourself. These feelings can come from various sources, as you've learned from this chapter. For example, being told by others that you're "too fat" or "too skinny" can chip away at your self-esteem, making you feel unattractive, unacceptable, or inadequate. When you tell yourself, "I look gross," it is often a sign that you feel like something is wrong with you. When we struggle to navigate and cope with these emotions in a healthy way, it becomes easy to blame the closest thing to us... our bodies.

By exploring the root cause of the issue, you can begin repairing your damaged body image. Here are some tips on how to process underlying emotions:

Identify triggers: Recognize situations, people, or environments that tend to evoke negative emotions from you. These triggers may include scrolling through social media, engaging in certain conversations, or participating in specific activities that emphasize appearance. For example, you may find that conversations with certain friends or family members frequently revolve around dieting or weight loss, triggering feelings of insecurity about your body. Identifying these triggers allows you to be more aware of situations that may harm your body image, empowering you to respond proactively.

Ask yourself "why": Once you've identified your triggers, take time to reflect on why they affect you. Ask yourself questions like, "Why do I feel this way?" or "What past experiences may be contributing to these feelings?" For example, if shopping for clothes triggers negative emotions about your body, don't immediately dismiss these feelings. Instead, take a moment to reflect on them. You might realize that they stem from past experiences of feeling judged or criticized while shopping with friends or family. Understanding these underlying emotions helps you understand why you feel negatively about your body and move toward a healthier approach.

Challenge negative thoughts: When negative thoughts about your body arise, challenge them with more realistic and compassionate perspectives. Instead of saying, "I hate how my body looks," reframe the statement to something more compassionate and empowering, such as "My body is strong and capable of amazing things." Remind yourself of your worth beyond physical appearance and focus on your strengths and qualities.

Addressing body image issues requires not only changing external factors but also shifting internal perspectives, beliefs, and emotions. Ultimately, healing body image involves fostering a positive relationship with yourself and embracing your unique beauty, both inside and out. As author Paulo Coelho once wrote, "Outer beauty is inner beauty made visible" (Coelho, 2013).

***

Now that you have a good understanding of how body image works, you are on your way toward healing and growth. The next step on this path is recognizing that recovery not only takes time and awareness but also kindness. In the next chapter, we'll discuss self-compassion and how you can cultivate a healthier relationship with your body through acts of kindness!

Pave the Road to Self Compassion

A *nd I said to my body, softly, "I want to be your friend." It took a long breath and replied, "I've been waiting my whole life for this."*
-Nayyirah Waheed

When Winnie Harlow was four years old, she was diagnosed with vitiligo, an autoimmune condition that causes white patches on the skin. This didn't faze little Winnie too much, though. She was a happy child with a loving and supportive family. Most importantly, they made it a point to celebrate her "differences" as an important part of who she was (The Drew Barrymore Show, 2020).

It was in third grade, after moving to a new school, that she started doubting herself. Her classmates avoided her, fearing they might "catch" her skin condition. The ostracism made Winnie feel incredibly lonely.

"I really wanted to make new friends. But kids called me a cow and mooed at me," she recalled (para. 3).

Throughout middle and high school, the bullying intensified. Every day during assembly, a boy would moo loudly at her, and everyone would laugh. While Winnie tried to defend herself sometimes, it only made the bullying worse. When her attempts to defend herself led to a physical altercation once, her mother immediately decided to transfer her to an alternative school. Free from her bullies, Winnie thrived academically.

In 2011, she received a message from a journalist asking her if she would be interested in sharing her experience in a YouTube video titled, *Vitiligo: A Skin Condition Not a Life Changer*. Winnie agreed. The journalist also told her that she was strikingly beautiful. This was the moment she first recognized that her unique look could be an asset. And so, she set her sights on modeling.

However, the industry seemed to be telling her she had the wrong idea. When she finally decided to pursue her goal and approached modeling agencies, she faced rejections one after another. Some agencies even suggested she might be better suited for the makeup department.

"It was an indirect hit aimed at my skin," Winnie recalled (para. 12).

Determined to embrace who she was, Winnie continued to share her story on social media platforms, challenging societal norms and inspiring others with vitiligo. When she was 19 years old, a casting director from *America's Next Top Model* spotted her on Facebook and invited her to audition for the show... and the rest was history! She placed sixth in the competition and her striking presence caught the attention of world-renowned photographers and designers. Winnie soon graced the campaigns of Desigual and Diesel, walked the runways of Madrid and New York Fashion Weeks, and stood alongside icons like Naomi Campbell, propelling her to supermodel status.

When she returned to her middle school to give a motivational speech, this is what Winnie had to say: "Looking back, I can see that the students who bullied me were just like me, trying to fit in" (Dailymail.com Reporter, 2015, para. 18).

Despite facing bullying and discrimination, Winnie refused to let these experiences define her self-worth. Instead, she embraced her uniqueness and recognized her own value beyond societal beauty standards. This is self-compassion in action, and it's what empowered Winnie to extend empathy and understanding not only to herself but also to others.

What Is Self-Compassion?

Self-compassion is the act of directing the kindness and empathy we typically show to others back toward ourselves. It's treating yourself with gentleness, understanding, and acceptance, especially in times of difficulty or suffering. There are three elements to self-compassion, according to psychologist and pioneer researcher Dr. Kristin Neff (2003).

First is self-kindness, which involves being supportive to yourself when facing stress or failure, rather than being harshly self-critical. For example, imagine you've worked hard on a project, but it didn't go as planned, resulting in a mistake that affected the outcome. Instead of berating yourself for the error and dwelling on what went wrong, you could take a moment to acknowledge your efforts and the challenges you faced. Remind yourself that everyone makes mistakes sometimes and that it's okay to not always get everything right. Reassure yourself that you're capable and that this setback doesn't define your worth or competence. Essentially, you treat yourself with the same kindness and patience that you would offer to a friend in a similar situation. By doing so, you train yourself to bounce back from disappointment with resilience and a renewed sense of determination.

Second is "common humanity" or the acknowledgment that suffering, failure, and imperfections are universal experiences shared by all humans, rather than viewing them as a personal struggle. For instance, you're at a gathering with friends, and you accidentally spill a drink on yourself. Instead of feeling embarrassed and thinking, *I'm so clumsy, everyone must think I'm a mess,* you remind yourself that spills happen to everyone from time to time. You laugh it off and clean up, knowing that your friends have likely experienced similar mishaps themselves.

This recognition of shared experiences helps you understand that struggles are something you share with others rather than something that sets you apart.

Third is mindfulness, which involves maintaining a balanced awareness of your thoughts, feelings, and experiences without becoming overwhelmed by them. It allows you to observe your thoughts and emotions objectively, giving you a sense of clarity and perspective. For example, you're at work, facing a challenging project with a tight deadline. As you dive into the task, you start to feel overwhelmed by the pressure to perform perfectly. Your mind begins to race with thoughts of potential mistakes and failures. Instead of getting caught up in this spiral of anxiety, mindfulness allows you to take a moment to pause. You recognize the pressure you're under, but you also acknowledge that it's a common experience many people face in their jobs. You are able to focus on the task at hand, break it down into manageable steps, and approach it with a calm and collected mindset. This allows you to work more effectively and make progress toward your goals, despite the initial feelings of stress and overwhelm.

Indeed, people who are pros at practicing self-compassion experience various benefits in terms of their mental health and well-being. Research shows that self-compassion helps in alleviating depression and anxiety, improving relationships, enhancing emotional awareness, managing stress, and reducing harmful behaviors like avoidance and rumination. Most notably, self-compassion is linked to reduced body shame and to lower levels of disordered eating (Haupt, 2023). As you can see, learning how to be kind to yourself is a crucial step toward healing your body image.

How Self-Compassion Impacts Body Image

When you look in the mirror, is the voice inside your head encouraging or mean? Life coach and author Lisa Hayes wrote, "Be careful what you say to yourself because you are listening" (Hayes, n.d.). Just like a garden needs nurturing, so too does your body deserve compassionate self-talk. Keep in mind that much of the discontent you feel toward your body stems from deep-rooted shame and feelings of inadequacy. When you let your inner critic run rampant, it's like pouring salt on a wound, exacerbating those feelings.

An interesting study by social psychologist Dr. Dacher Keltner (2012) proposes that humans have evolved to be compassionate. Our ancestors embraced kindness to form bonds with tribes and raise children, increasing their likelihood of survival. These traits were then passed onto future generations. Thus, if compassion is part of our DNA, why is it often difficult to be kind to ourselves?

This is because while compassion may be inherent, practicing it requires overcoming various barriers, including beliefs formed during our upbringing. Research suggests that around 40% of people grew up developing insecure attachments to their parents, which might make them uncomfortable with the idea of being kind to themselves. In a secure relationship, parents are good at understanding their child's feelings and creating a sense of safety. However, in insecure relationships, parents might not always respond kindly to their child's feelings, which can make the child anxious (Benner, 2022).

For example, if you felt ignored or were told to toughen up by your parents every time you felt sad as a child, you might grow up thinking expressing sadness makes you weak and, therefore, unlikable. Consequently, every time you receive compassion from yourself or others as an adult, you may believe that's how you are perceived.

Modern society has also instilled in us beliefs that can hinder our ability to be kind to ourselves. Here are some common ones:

Being hard on yourself will motivate you: Many people hold the misconception that being hard on themselves serves as a driving force to achieve success and excel in various aspects of life. They may believe that being gentle and caring with themselves would lead to complacency or laziness, resulting in stagnation or failure. However, research has shown that negative self-talk actually does the opposite. It reduces motivation by amplifying feelings of stress and helplessness. It also leads to limited thinking and perfectionism, which can hinder progress toward achieving goals (Scott, 2023).

Self-compassion is the same as self-pity or self-indulgence: Some people fear that showing themselves kindness during tough times may lead to self-pity or be perceived as self-indulgence. However, self-compassion is not the same as these. Here are some tips on how to tell the difference:

Self-indulgence involves excessive focus on short-term pleasure or gratification without considering the long-term consequences. For example, despite knowing you need to study for an important test, you decide to binge-watch your favorite TV show instead, ignoring the impact it will have on your academic performance. In contrast, self-compassion in this scenario would involve acknowledging the desire for short-term pleasure but prioritizing long-term well-being. Instead of harshly criticizing yourself for the urge to procrastinate, you offer understanding and make a conscious decision to make time for both relaxation and study.

Self-pity involves dwelling on one's own misfortunes or difficulties without actively seeking solutions or taking responsibility for improvement. For example, you continually complain about your workload but make no effort to communicate with your supervisor or find ways to manage your tasks more effectively. Self-compassion in this scenario would involve acknowledging the challenges you're facing while taking proactive steps to address the situation (Gourlay, 2020).

Self-compassion isn't important: Many individuals struggle with self-compassion simply because they grew up in an environment where it wasn't emphasized or taught. If you are like me, the concept of self-compassion was not taught to you at home or in school. Instead, you grew up seeing Western society value toughness and resilience above all else. Additionally, societal norms often praise little girls for prioritizing the needs of others, expecting them to be self-sacrificing and nurturing—something not typically imposed on young boys. As a result, many of us grew up without the necessary skills to prioritize our own well-being, leading to feelings of guilt whenever we try to do so.

By shifting your focus away from nitpicking your appearance to being compassionate to yourself as you are in the present moment, you open up mental space to pursue your goals and live a more fulfilling life.

Self-Compassion Strategies

Embracing self-compassion is easier said than done. However, when paired with actionable strategies, it becomes more tangible and can evolve into a habit. So, now that you have a good understanding of the concept and the challenges involved, it's time to incorporate self-compassion practices into your daily life! By doing so, you can build a healthier, more loving relationship with your body. As author and educator Sharon Salzberg puts it, "Self-compassion is like a muscle. The more we practice flexing it, especially when life doesn't go exactly according to plan, the stronger and more resilient our compassion muscle becomes" (Salzberg, 2017).

Strategy #1: Beautiful Body Affirmations

Affirmations are short, positive statements that you regularly repeat to yourself for empowerment. You can use them not just to practice self-compassion, but also for various purposes such as motivation, resilience, stress reduction, and more. While affirmations are often associated with spirituality in our culture, the science behind them has actually been extensively studied.

Its effectiveness is closely tied to the concept of neuroplasticity in the brain. Neuroplasticity refers to the brain's ability to change and adapt throughout our lives. Think of your brain as a forest, with many different paths you can take. Each time you repeat an affirmation, it's like walking along a new footpath. At first, the path might be overgrown and difficult to see, but with each use, the path becomes more defined. Similarly, when you repeat affirmations regularly, it's like exercising a muscle in your brain. Just as physical exercise strengthens your muscles, affirmations strengthen the neural pathways associated with positive thoughts and beliefs (Raypole, 2020). This is what transforms the brain from instantly generating negative thoughts, such as *I look terrible*, to cultivating more positive ones like, *I am beautiful just the way I am*.

Research has shown that affirmations offer a wide array of benefits, such as improving self-control, encouraging healthier habits, supporting behavior change, and even reducing excessive smartphone use. Most notably, affirmations are effective in cultivating empathy and compassion (Bredehoft, 2023).

So, how do you use affirmations effectively? Here are five tips:

Be specific: Tailor your affirmations to address specific areas or goals you want to work on. For example, since we are aiming to heal body image, your affirmation could be, "Every part of my body is deserving of kindness and respect."

Use the present tense: Phrase your affirmations as if you already possess the qualities or achievements you desire. This helps shift your mindset from longing for something in the future to embodying it in the present moment. For instance, instead of saying, "One day, I will feel good about my body," say, "I am grateful for my body and all it does for me each day."

Keep them positive: Affirmations evoke feelings of empowerment and motivation, driving you toward your goals, so they should be focused on what you want to attract or achieve, rather than what you want to avoid or eliminate. Instead of saying, "I don't want to hate how I look anymore," which keeps the focus on the undesired state, you could affirm, "I love my body."

Visualize: As you repeat your affirmations, imagine yourself already embodying the qualities or achievements you desire. This adds a powerful visual component to your practice. For instance, if your affirmation is "I am confident and comfortable in my own skin," picture yourself standing tall, radiating self-assurance, and embracing your unique beauty. By vividly imagining yourself in this empowered state, you reinforce the message of your affirmation and strengthen your belief in its truth.

Repeat them regularly: Consistency is key when it comes to affirmations. Repeat them daily, ideally multiple times a day, to reinforce positive thinking patterns and rewire your subconscious mind. Many people find it helpful to incorporate affirmations into their mornings, either as soon as they wake up or while getting ready for the day. Others prefer to practice in bed before sleep. Regardless of the timing, the key is to make affirmations a regular part of your routine.

With these guidelines in mind, you're ready to begin! While you can always create your own affirmations, feel free to use the examples provided here to kick-start your practice:

My body is strong, resilient, and capable of achieving great things.

I am grateful for all the amazing things my body allows me to do every day.

I celebrate my body's unique shape and size, knowing that it is perfect just as it is.

Every imperfection on my body tells a story of resilience and growth.

I honor and respect my body by nourishing it with healthy foods and movement.

My body is a temple of love and deserves to be treated with kindness and compassion.

I embrace my natural beauty and radiate confidence from within.

I release all negative thoughts about my body and replace them with love and acceptance.

I am worthy of love and respect.

My worth is not determined by my weight or size; I am valuable just as I am.

I trust my body's wisdom and listen to its signals with love and understanding.

Every part of my body is unique and beautiful in its own way.

I am grateful for the journey my body has taken me on and the experiences it has allowed me to have.

I choose to focus on the things I love about my body.

My body is my greatest ally, supporting me in all aspects of my life.

I am confident in my skin and embrace my individuality with pride.

I let go of comparison and embrace my own path to health and happiness.

I am worthy of self-care and prioritize my well-being above all else.

I trust my body's ability to heal and regenerate, both physically and emotionally.

I am enough just as I am, and I deserve to feel confident and comfortable in my own skin.

It may take some time to get used to incorporating affirmations into your routine, but try to be as consistent as you can. Remember, it's also important to maintain confidence in the effectiveness of your affirmations and to align your actions with your statements.

Strategy #2: Self-Care Rituals

The term "self-care" has become a buzzword nowadays in the media. It is often portrayed as treating yourself to fancy spa days, expensive skincare, or shopping sprees. While there is nothing inherently wrong with indulging in these activities, companies and brands that market their products and services as essential for self-care do contribute to a few misconceptions about it.

The truth is, self-care is more than just a one-time treat or owning a trendy product. It involves regularly doing things that make you feel good inside and out. It means proactively taking care of your body, mind, and emotions every day in a way that suits you best. So, while treating yourself is nice, real self-care is about doing things that help you maintain balance and happiness in the long run—and that can look different for everyone!

However, it is also true that having body image issues can make self-care quite challenging. When you harbor negative feelings toward something, like your body, it becomes harder to muster the motivation for nurturing it. The good news is that self-care isn't only reserved for those who already feel confident in their bodies! You don't have to wait until you love every inch of yourself before you start prioritizing caring for it. In fact, it is often those who struggle the most with body image who stand to benefit the most from some much-needed TLC.

A survey revealed that while seven out of ten Americans recognize the importance of self-care, only about 6.7% actively practice it on a regular basis. Various studies have shed light on the reasons behind this. Firstly, self-care is often not viewed as a priority in our fast-paced world. Secondly, it is commonly perceived as expensive or time-consuming. Thirdly, some people feel guilty when taking time for themselves because they view it as selfish (Tee-Melegrito, 2023).

However, research consistently demonstrates the many benefits of self-care, including reduced stress, lower levels of anxiety and depression, enhanced focus, and increased overall happiness and energy. Prioritizing self-care has also been linked to a decreased risk of developing serious health conditions such as heart disease, stroke, and cancer. Moreover, self-care has been observed to help us connect to what matters most to us and, thus, allows us to pursue a more meaningful life (Glowiak, 2024). Therefore, it's essential to recognize that self-care isn't a luxury but a basic necessity for overall well-being.

That being said, here is a simple guide on how you can create effective self-care rituals:

Take a moment to reflect on areas of your life that could use more care and attention. Consider your physical, mental, emotional, and spiritual well-being. For example, if you often feel overwhelmed, anxious, or sad, it might be a sign that you need to focus on your emotional health.

Make a list of activities that make you feel happy, relaxed, and rejuvenated. These can include anything from going for a walk in nature, practicing mindfulness or meditation, reading a book, taking a hot bath, or spending time with loved ones. Remember to focus on how these activities make you feel rather than how they make you look.

Set aside dedicated time in your schedule for self-care activities. Treat this time as non-negotiable, just like any other important appointment or commitment.

Start small. Begin with manageable activities that you can easily incorporate into your daily or weekly routine, like taking a short walk around your neighborhood or spending 10 minutes reading before bed. Starting small allows you to build momentum and gradually expand your self-care practices over time.

Set boundaries. Learn to say "no" to activities or commitments that drain your energy or cause unnecessary stress. Setting boundaries is an essential aspect of self-care, as it allows you to prioritize your well-being and protect your mental and emotional health.

Seek support. Don't hesitate to reach out to friends, family, or a professional therapist for encouragement on your self-care journey. Surrounding yourself with a supportive network can provide valuable insight, accountability, and motivation.

Remember that self-care looks different for everyone, so it's important to experiment until you find what activities truly nourish and replenish you.

Strategy #3: Journaling

Journaling is the practice of regularly writing down your thoughts, feelings, experiences, and reflections in a notebook or journal. It can take many forms, including free-form writing, structured prompts, bullet points, or even artistic expression like drawing or collage. Journaling is a powerful tool for self-expression, self-discovery, and personal growth. It enables you to explore your innermost thoughts and feelings, gain clarity on experiences, track progress toward goals, and cultivate gratitude and mindfulness.

Additionally, journaling offers numerous health benefits! Research shows that journaling can reduce sick days, lower anxiety and blood pressure, prevent obsessive thinking, improve awareness, enhance lung and liver function, and promote better mental health. Most importantly, it can boost self-esteem, which is extremely important in healing body image (Sutton, 2018). Consider these journaling tips before you begin:

Set aside dedicated time: Choose a specific time of day when you can consistently devote a few minutes to journaling. Whether it's first thing in the morning, during lunch break, or before bed, find a time that works best for you.

Use prompts: If you're unsure what to write about, consider using journaling prompts to spark inspiration. Prompts can range from simple questions to thought-provoking statements or themes to explore. Websites, books, and journaling apps often offer a variety of prompts to choose from. Some free apps you can explore include Reflectly, Happyfeed, and Longwalks (Borges & Ryu, 2023).

Keep it simple: Your journaling practice doesn't have to be elaborate or time-consuming. Start with just a few sentences or bullet points if that feels more manageable. The goal is consistency, not perfection.

Write freely: Try not to worry too much about grammar, spelling, or punctuation. Let your thoughts flow freely onto the page without judgment or self-editing. Your journal is a safe space for you to express yourself authentically.

Experiment with formats: Explore different journaling formats to find what works best for you. This could include traditional written journaling, digital journaling apps, voice recordings, or even visual journaling with drawings or collages.

Reflect and review: Take time to reflect on your journal entries periodically. Notice any patterns, insights, or changes in your thoughts and feelings over time. This reflection can help deepen your self-awareness and personal growth.

Now that you're all set, here are 20 journaling prompts to help you get started:

How do you currently feel about your body? Describe your thoughts and emotions honestly.

Imagine a world where beauty standards didn't exist. What would your relationship with your body look like in this ideal scenario?

Are there any specific body parts you struggle to accept or appreciate? Explore the origins of these feelings.

How do societal standards and media representations of beauty influence your perception of your body?

Write a letter to your body, expressing gratitude for all it does for you.

Think about a role model or influencer who promotes body positivity. How does their message resonate with you?

Recall a time when someone made a hurtful comment about your appearance. How did it impact your self-image?

List three things you love about your body and explain why they are meaningful to you.

Reflect on a time when you felt most confident in your body. What were you doing?

How do you define beauty beyond physical appearance? Explore the qualities that make you unique and valuable.

Explore a childhood memory related to body image. How has this memory influenced your perception of your body as an adult?

Write about a time when you compared yourself to others and felt inadequate. How can you practice self-compassion in these moments?

Consider the role of self-care in nurturing a positive body image. What self-care practices make you feel most connected to your body?

Explore the connection between your body image and your mental health. How does your perception of your body affect your mood and well-being?

Reflect on cultural or familial influences on your body image. How have these factors shaped your relationship with your body?

Write a list of affirmations to boost your body confidence. Repeat these affirmations daily.

Describe a positive experience you've had that challenged negative beliefs about your body. What did you learn from this experience?

Reflect on the language you use when talking about your body. How can you shift to more compassionate and empowering language?

Write a letter to your younger self, offering words of encouragement.

Imagine your future self feeling confident and empowered in your body. What steps can you take today to move closer to this vision?

Be patient with yourself and approach journaling with compassion and curiosity. Keep in mind that it's okay if it takes time to find your rhythm or if some days feel more challenging than others.

***

By treating yourself with kindness, understanding, and acceptance, you can learn to embrace your body as it is and appreciate it for all it does for you. Now that you've explored the important role of self-compassion in healing body image, it's time to take the next step! In the next chapter, we'll explore the empowering concept of body positivity and how it can help you cultivate a more inclusive mindset toward yourself and others.

Accepting Body Positivity

*O*ne day I decided that I was beautiful, and so I carried out my life as if I was a beautiful girl. It doesn't have anything to do with how the world perceives you. What matters is what you see.
-Gabourey Sidibe

In a blog post for *The Wild Woman*, Colleen Large shared how she stumbled upon the body positivity movement. For years, Colleen yearned for a thinner body and constantly hated herself for not having one. She had always been athletic and the tallest in every class, which meant she was often perceived as the biggest. Even during the years when Colleen lost weight, she claimed she never felt "thin enough."

However, in her mid-twenties, Colleen reached a turning point. She finally realized that living in a constant state of self-loathing was neither sustainable nor fulfilling for her. The daily discomfort of hating herself prompted her to make a change. "Something clicked, and I chose to start taking steps towards loving my body and loving myself because I really couldn't take it anymore. I was so tired of hating myself," Colleen shared (Large, 2022, para. 13).

She turned to social media for encouragement and found the body positivity movement, which was only starting to take shape at that time. As she engaged with the movement's content, she gained awareness of crucial concepts like thin privilege, fatphobia, and the detrimental effects of the diet industry. Through exposure to diverse representations of bodies, particularly via plus-size influencers on various platforms, Colleen began to challenge the notion that beauty was exclusive to one body size.

Over the course of several years, Colleen actively worked on cultivating self-love and confidence. She started a blog and shared outfit ideas on social media, gradually embracing her body and celebrating its beauty. What once felt like a daunting task—taking photos and being seen in public—became a source of joy and empowerment for Colleen. Now, she proudly proclaims that every woman, no matter what shape or size, can be stylish and attractive! "I want more than anything for people to feel what I feel, that my body is good and that all bodies are good," Colleen wrote (para. 21).

Colleen's story is a powerful reminder that embracing one's body is a radical act of self-love. Body positivity played a significant role in her journey, and you've probably heard the term before, but what exactly is it?

What Is Body Positivity?

Body positivity is both a social movement and mindset that encourages people to accept and love their bodies as they are, regardless of shape, size, or appearance. It challenges societal beauty standards and norms by promoting inclusivity and diversity in representations of beauty. It also advocates for recognizing the intrinsic value of every body, firmly rejecting body shaming, and nurturing a positive body image across all genders, races, sizes, abilities, and identities.

For context, the movement emerged in the 1960s as a response to rampant weight bias and shaming. Its aim was to dismantle the connection between weight and self-worth, asserting that everyone deserves dignity, respect, and fair treatment regardless of the number on the scale. It campaigned for positive change, particularly within the medical field, challenging the idea that weight directly reflects one's health or hygiene standards (Fuller, 2022b). Ultimately, body positivity aims to empower individuals to feel confident, comfortable, and proud of their bodies.

To understand what it is, let's first clarify what it's not. Here are some key myths and misconceptions surrounding body positivity.

Myth #1: Body Positivity Is Anti-Health

The misconception that body positivity is merely an excuse to promote unhealthy habits, such as overeating or neglecting physical activity, stems from a misunderstanding of the movement's core principles. In reality, body positivity promotes holistic well-being and self-care.

Advocates of body positivity emphasize the importance of cultivating a positive relationship with one's body, which involves nurturing it with nutritious food, engaging in joyful movement, and prioritizing overall wellness. In fact, according to a report, discussions around body positivity between 2017 and 2020 predominantly featured the keyword "self-care" (Reid, 2020).

Rather than promoting unhealthy habits, body positivity encourages individuals to listen to their bodies, honor their needs, and adopt sustainable lifestyle practices that support their health and happiness. It emphasizes self-compassion and acceptance, recognizing that everyone's journey to health looks different and that true well-being extends beyond physical appearance.

Myth #2: Body Positivity Is Exclusively for Plus-Size Women

As we've previously discussed, body positivity has its roots in pushing back against fat shaming, which may explain why there's a misconception that it is exclusively a movement for plus-size individuals. Furthermore, when it started gaining traction on social media, the pioneering activists and influencers were predominantly women, because we are the ones who have faced significant societal stigma and discrimination. This marginalization has led to a greater need for empowerment and visibility, but it also resulted in some misconceptions about the intended audience of the body positivity movement.

In reality, body positivity is not even about weight and gender; it advocates for the acceptance and celebration of all bodies, regardless of size, shape, sexual orientation, or identity. People of color, gender nonconforming individuals, and those with visible disabilities or chronic illnesses are just a few examples of who could benefit from body positivity the most, as these groups often face harsh criticism, discrimination, and stigma. By perpetuating the myth that body positivity is exclusively for one gender or weight category, we overlook the diverse range of people who can benefit from the movement's principles of self-love, acceptance, and inclusivity.

Myth #3: Body Positivity Is Focused Solely on Physical Appearance

Some people think body positivity is just about how we look, but it's so much more than that. Body positivity is all about loving and accepting ourselves for who we are, inside and out. It's about feeling good about our bodies, no matter the shape, size, or appearance. It encourages us to take care of our mental and emotional well-being by being kind to ourselves and embracing our unique experiences.

Body positivity also challenges the unrealistic beauty standards society puts on us. It encourages us to question and resist harmful messages about beauty, promoting inclusivity and diversity in representation, so that everyone feels seen and valued.

Kanika Mukhija, a big supporter of body positivity, sums it up perfectly: "To me, body positivity is loving each and every body type and image. I take care of myself by giving my body the exercise and nutrition it deserves. I no longer bother about the societal standards" (Siddhanti, 2021, para. 15).

Myth #4: Body Positivity Means You Have to Love Every Part of Your Body

Thinking that every body-positive supporter loves every aspect of their bodies without exception oversimplifies the movement and overlooks the complexity of human experience. In truth, body positivity is about embracing and accepting your body as a whole by recognizing its inherent worth and value beyond superficial appearances. This doesn't necessarily mean loving all parts of your body unconditionally every minute of the day; rather, it involves acknowledging and honoring your body's individuality.

It's normal for anyone to have areas of their body that they may feel less confident about or struggle to accept. Body positivity encourages self-compassion and self-acceptance, even in the face of these insecurities. Moreover, body positivity recognizes that everyone's journey to self-acceptance is unique. It's okay to have days where you struggle with body image—it's all part of the process! The goal of body positivity is not perfection or unconditional love, but rather learning to appreciate and care for your body in a holistic way, regardless of how it looks and how you feel about it at the moment.

Myth #5: Body Positivity Is Just a Social Media Trend

Because body positivity is all over social media, some might think it's just a passing trend. But actually, it's been around for decades, even before the internet! While sites like Instagram and Tiktok have helped spread the message, body positivity is about way more than hashtags and online activism.

In truth, body positivity advocates for systemic change in how society perceives and treats bodies. This means standing up against appearance-based discrimination and stigma. It also seeks to create a culture of inclusivity, where all bodies are celebrated and valued, and that's not achieved by only sharing cute pics with inspiring captions on social media—although that is one part of it!

In fact, the fashion and beauty industries, which have significant if not the most considerable influence on body perception, historically dismissed the movement's calls for diversity and inclusion until recently. As the influence of body positivity grew and consumer attitudes changed, numerous global brands have begun introducing expanded size ranges to cater to a broader variety of body types. Major companies like Forever 21, Calvin Klein, and even Victoria's Secret have embraced this initiative by offering more size options to their customers (Pratik, 2022).

Additionally, we are now seeing beauty brands making efforts to welcome and represent customers of all skin shades and gender identities. For example, Rihanna's Fenty Beauty line set a new standard in 2017 with its 40-foundation range. Influential figures like Yara Shahidi, Sasha Lane, and Tracee Ellis Ross are also redefining Hollywood glamor by embracing their natural hair textures, inspiring change in the hair care industry (Shapiro, 2018).

Body positivity aims to make real, lasting changes in the way we think about bodies, and that's exactly what it's doing.

How to Be Body Positive

A study found that exposure to body-positive posts on social media made people feel better about their bodies and boosted their mood. This impact was consistent among women with differing pre-existing beliefs about beauty (Alleva, 2021). Essentially, no matter what you thought before, body positivity can improve overall well-being and help you feel good about yourself.

There are countless ways to cultivate body positivity; it's all about finding what works for you. Here are some suggestions to help you kick off your journey:

Stop giving numbers too much power: Numerous studies have shown that weighing yourself frequently can negatively affect how you feel about yourself, your body, and your eating habits (Pacanowski et al., 2016). Aside from the scale, we can let numbers rule our lives—calories, dress size, body measurements, and more! Instead of fixating on these, try to focus on how you feel, your overall health, and the things that truly make you happy. Remember, you're more than just a number, and freeing your mind from continuously weighing and tracking will allow it to focus on more fulfilling and joyful activities.

Gracefully accept a compliment: When someone compliments you, simply say "thank you" and take it in. If someone says, "Wow, you look amazing!" Resist the urge to deflect or downplay the compliment; instead, allow yourself to bask in the positivity. Rather than responding with, "Oh, I don't know, I feel kind of bloated," or "Thanks, but I'm actually not feeling great," try saying: "Thank you so much! That means a lot to me." By accepting the compliment and allowing yourself to receive it with gratitude, you are reinforcing positive self-esteem and encouraging a healthier mindset toward yourself and your body.

Move your body in ways that feel good: Exercise shouldn't feel like a chore or punishment, but rather a celebration of what your body is capable of. Whether it's dancing to your favorite music, going for a walk in nature, practicing yoga, or playing a sport you love, find movement that nourishes both your body and soul. Focus on how exercise makes you feel rather than how many calories you're burning or what your body looks like.

Practice mindfulness: Take a few moments throughout your day to pause and check in with yourself. Close your eyes, take a few deep breaths, and focus your attention inward. Notice any physical sensations, emotions, or thoughts that arise without judgment or criticism. Allow yourself to fully experience the present moment, accepting whatever arises with compassion and curiosity. You can also integrate mindfulness practices such as deep breathing exercises or meditation into your daily routine. By incorporating mindfulness into your daily life, you can develop a greater awareness of your body's needs and cues.

Dress comfortably: When your clothes don't fit well, it can make you feel uneasy about your body. Studies reveal that wearing uncomfortable clothes can affect your focus and confidence (Lees, 2020). Instead, opt for clothes that let you move freely and show your true self. You don't have to compromise style for comfort! Whether it's a comfy sweater, a breezy dress, or your go-to jeans, choose outfits that make you feel relaxed and self-assured. This way, you'll feel more comfortable in your own skin.

Remember, body positivity is about embracing and accepting yourself exactly as you are. It takes time, and it's okay to have setbacks. The important thing is to keep showing yourself love and compassion every step of the way.

How Social Media Impacts Body Image

We can't discuss body image without addressing the impact of social media. With approximately 3.6 billion users globally, social media holds considerable influence over our perception of beauty in today's world.

The constant stream of images online leads us to compare ourselves and view our bodies through a different lens. Numerous studies have revealed that social media is closely associated with feelings of body dissatisfaction and the development of unhealthy eating habits (Fleps, 2021).

Additionally, social media provides a platform for anonymous or semi-anonymous interactions, making it easier for users to engage in negative behaviors without facing immediate consequences. This anonymity can embolden people to express hurtful or derogatory comments about others' appearances without considering the impact of their words. Moreover, the instantaneous and widespread nature of social media allows hurtful comments or images to quickly reach a large audience, amplifying their impact and making them difficult to escape.

However, cutting out social media altogether might not be doable for most of us, especially in today's extremely connected world. So, now that we know how it can affect our well-being and body image, the next smart move is to take charge of how we use it.

Curating a Body-Positive Feed

Transforming your feed with uplifting content, diverse perspectives, and supportive communities allows you to reclaim your space on social media and cultivate a healthier relationship with your body. Rather than feeling down with every scroll, intentionally curating your feed encourages you to embrace your uniqueness.

Here are some tips on how to have a more body-positive social media feed:

Follow body-positive accounts: Seek out influencers, activists, and organizations that promote body positivity, self-love, and acceptance. Look for accounts who celebrate diverse bodies and challenge mainstream beauty standards. If you're not sure how to begin, check out the hashtags your favorite creators are using! If you come across a new account that you connect with and lifts your spirits, don't hesitate to hit that follow button.

Diversify your feed: Follow accounts representing a range of body types, ethnicities, genders, and abilities. Exposure to diverse perspectives can broaden your understanding of beauty and help you appreciate the uniqueness of all bodies.

Avoid triggering content: On the flip side, you should also unfollow accounts that consistently make you feel inadequate or trigger negative thoughts about your body. If unfollowing isn't possible, consider muting. This may include accounts that promote unrealistic beauty standards or perpetuate harmful diet culture. If you're concerned about offending anyone, remember that your settings are private, and it's important to prioritize your own well-being in your decisions.

Set boundaries: Be mindful of the time you spend on social media and observe how it affects your mood and self-esteem negatively. Consider setting limits on your screen time or taking breaks from scrolling when needed. Instead, engage in real-life activities that allow you to focus on what truly matters to you.

Engage positively: The more you engage with specific content, the more of it you'll see—and this can work to your advantage! If you're tired of seeing posts about diets or unrealistic beauty standards, for instance, avoid interacting with them. Instead, like, comment, and share body-positive content that resonates with you and uplifts your spirits. Engaging with such posts not only supports content creators but also helps spread messages of body positivity to a wider audience.

Be mindful of your own content: If you feel compelled, share your journey toward body acceptance and self-love with others. Your authentic experiences and positive messages have the power to inspire and empower those in your online community. Don't hold back because of fear of judgment from others; embracing vulnerability is a powerful exercise in self-acceptance.

By implementing these tips, you can curate a social media feed that nourishes your soul, fosters body positivity, and celebrates the diversity of human bodies!

Why Your Body Deserves Love

Loving your body is a lifelong practice, and it's not always going to be easy. However, understanding why it's important can provide you with the motivation to persevere. So, if you need a little pep talk, here are a few compelling reasons why it's totally worth it.

Firstly, your body is unique! From the curve of your smile to the texture of your hair, there is no one else in the world quite like you—unless, perhaps, you have an identical twin, but even then! Embracing your individuality isn't just empowering; it's what makes you special.

Secondly, your body does so much for you every day. It's there for you through every dance move and every hug with friends. Your body is like your own personal superhero, always by your side, showing up for you unconditionally whenever you need it.

Lastly, your body is incredibly resilient; it allows you to bounce back even when times are tough. So, when you show your body love, you're also extending an act of kindness to yourself.

Reframing Negative Body Statements and Opinions

One powerful way to love your body is by paying attention to what you believe about it. Changing your negative thoughts is key to feeling more positive about your body. Yet, sometimes, we don't even realize we're being hard on ourselves or that we are holding onto harmful beliefs. With that said, let's explore some of the most damaging thoughts, so we can start turning them around!

"I Hate My..."

Whether it's "I hate my arms," "I hate my thighs," or any other body part, focusing too much on what you see as flaws can lead to dissatisfaction and can totally mess with your relationship with your body. To reframe this damaging thought, try shifting your focus from what you dislike to what your body does for you.

For example, instead of saying, "I hate my stomach," you could say, "My stomach allows me to enjoy delicious meals with friends and family." By acknowledging the functionality and strength of your body, you can cultivate a more positive relationship with it.

"I'd Be Happier if I Were..."

Feeling like you'd be happier if you were thinner, taller, or had a different body shape is something many of us struggle with. But dwelling on these thoughts can really take a toll on your mental health and self-esteem. That's why it's important to shift your focus to what truly matters: your unique qualities, strengths, and the things you love about yourself. Celebrate your body for all it does for you, from the strength to go for a run to the flexibility to try a new yoga pose.

For example, instead of saying "I'd be happier if I were thinner," reframe it to "I am worthy of happiness and love regardless of my size." This shift in perspective acknowledges your inherent worth and focuses on cultivating inner happiness rather than chasing external validation. Remember, happiness and self-worth aren't tied to a number on the scale or a specific body shape!

"I Can't Wear That Because I'm Not..."

Any thought that blames your body for not being able to do or have something, like wearing certain clothes, can be really harmful. It perpetuates the idea that only certain body types can enjoy certain things, which can lead to feelings of inadequacy and shame. Reframing this thought involves recognizing that style is not limited by size and that everyone deserves to wear clothes that make them feel confident and comfortable.

So, instead of saying "I can't wear that because I'm not...," try thinking, "I can wear whatever I want because my body deserves to feel comfortable and confident in any outfit." Then, choose clothing that reflects your personal style, regardless of your size or shape. Keep in mind that fashion is for everyone, and beauty comes in all shapes and sizes.

"Everything I Wear Makes Me Look Bad"

Even the most confident person you know will have days when they feel insecure. Some days, it just feels like nothing fits quite right, or every outfit leaves you feeling uneasy or unsure. During these challenging moments, rather than criticizing yourself, it's important to shift your focus toward gratitude for your body and its unique qualities.

Whenever the thought "Everything I wear makes me look bad" creeps in, challenge it with affirmations that highlight your worth and beauty. For example, say to yourself, "I appreciate my body for all it does for me, regardless of how clothes look on me." Remind yourself that you are more than just your appearance, you are also how you carry yourself and how you choose to show up in the world and for others.

Cultivating Love for Your Body

Love is both a noun and a verb. You practice it by showing compassion through both intention and actions. That's why, after reframing your thoughts, it's time to express love for your body through tangible gestures. Here are some strategies you can incorporate into your day-to-day life to cultivate a more positive and loving view of your body:

Be generous with compliments: By complimenting others, you not only spread positivity but also train your mind to notice and appreciate beauty in all its forms. This practice encourages you to see the uniqueness and value in others, which can translate into seeing those same qualities in yourself.

Focus on health, not weight: Shifting the focus from weight to overall health helps you develop a more holistic understanding of well-being. By prioritizing healthy habits such as nutritious eating, regular exercise, and stress management, you learn to appreciate your body's capabilities and strengths rather than fixating on its appearance.

Embrace your stretch marks: Stretch marks often appear during periods of growth, such as puberty or pregnancy, and are a natural part of the body's development. Instead of viewing stretch marks as flaws, see them as beautiful reminders of growth and change! Embrace them as unique features that tell your story and reflect your resilience.

Make space for both bigger and smaller bodies: Recognize that bodies come in all shapes and sizes, and each one is worthy of love and respect. Challenge societal norms that dictate certain body types as more desirable than others. Celebrate diversity by appreciating the beauty of all bodies, whether they're larger, smaller, or anywhere in between. By embracing body diversity, you can foster a more inclusive and accepting view of yourself and others.

Be selective with the people you surround yourself with: Being around positive, supportive people creates an environment where self-love and body acceptance are celebrated. When you're surrounded by people who uplift and encourage you, it becomes easier to internalize those messages and view yourself through a more compassionate lens.

Stop comparing yourself to others: Comparing yourself to others breeds feelings of inadequacy and self-doubt, ultimately harming your self-esteem. Instead, focus on your own journey and give yourself the space to appreciate your unique qualities and accomplishments without comparing them to others, whether in real life, online, or other media sources.

Engage in body-positive activities: Seek out activities and hobbies that promote body positivity and self-expression. Attend workshops or events focused on body acceptance, join body-positive communities online or in-person, and participate in creative endeavors like art, writing, or dance that celebrate diverse bodies and perspectives. Surrounding yourself with like-minded people and engaging in body-positive activities can uplift your spirits and reinforce positive self-image.

Celebrate yourself: Take pride in your accomplishments and milestones, both big and small. Whether you excel in academics, sports, career, or personal passions, acknowledge your hard work and achievements with pride. Recognize that your worth extends far beyond physical attributes and honor the unique qualities and talents that truly make you who you are!

Normalize "bad" days: Feeling insecure about your body is something many people go through, and it doesn't mean you're failing in any way. No matter your age, gender, or appearance, we all struggle with body image at different times in our lives. Instead of thinking of body image distress as wrong or embarrassing, see it as a normal reaction to society's unrealistic beauty standards. Understanding and accepting these feelings as part of being human can ease the pressure to be "perfect" and help you be kinder to yourself.

Incorporating these strategies into your daily life can empower you to cultivate a more positive and loving relationship with your body. Remember that progress takes time and effort, so be patient. We've been conditioned for most of our lives not to like ourselves, so the journey toward self-love won't happen overnight. What's important is to keep trying.

***

By putting into practice what you've learned in this chapter, you're steadily moving toward changing your mindset from self-criticism to self-appreciation. But our journey is far from over! In the next chapter, we'll explore confidence and how to embrace your body wholeheartedly. It's not just about acceptance anymore—it's about empowerment and celebration!

Rewrite the
Narrative

*C*onfidence is the only key. I can't think of any better
representation of beauty than someone who is unafraid to be
herself. -Emma Stone

In her website, Lindsey shared that she started feeling insecure
about her body at a young age. As a child competitive swimmer, she
found her focus shifting from performance to appearance when one
day, she noticed a small dimple on her left thigh, which she made
herself remember to cover with her hand at all times.

By the time Lindsey reached adolescence, her insecurities had
intensified. She diligently documented weight-loss goals and food
intake in her journals, driven by the relentless pursuit of the
ideal body depicted by the teen magazines she owned. She never
questioned her behavior because it seemed normal among her
friends, and the media portrayed dieting and fitness as normal.

"We were all middle-class white girls from Idaho, with happy,
successful families of all shapes and sizes, but we all shared the
deep-seated idea that the only way to attain happiness, popularity, and

love was to be as thin and beautiful as possible," Lindsey shared (para. 4).

It wasn't until Lindsey's college years that she began to challenge her beliefs. Through a journalism class, she learned to dissect media messages and recognize their role in creating insecurities for young girls. This newfound awareness allowed her to reflect on her actions and cultivate true confidence. It even ignited a passion within her to advocate for body positivity. She realized that many of her insecurities had subconsciously affected her life.

Reflecting, Lindsey wrote: "When I became more worried about the dimple in my thigh than my race time, I stopped excelling as a swimmer. When I am fixated on keeping my clothes in the most flattering position and everything sucked in just right, I can't concentrate on anything else at all. I was overwhelmed just thinking of the number of activities I could have excelled at, the relationships I could have cultivated, the goals I could have pursued if I hadn't spent so much of my life preoccupied with the way I looked" (Kite & Kite, 2016, para. 8).

We all have them—those little nagging doubts about our bodies, the insecurities that whisper in our ears, telling us we're not good enough. But what if, instead of feeling weighed down by self-doubt, you could step into a space of confidence? Yes, it's possible! And it all starts with redefining how you view yourself and your body.

Exploring Your Body Insecurities

Maybe you wish you were a few pounds lighter or a few inches taller. Perhaps you want your skin to be clearer or smoother. Or maybe it's about features like your nose, your thighs, or the shape of your stomach. These are just a few examples of the countless insecurities that many women grapple with every day. And while they might seem harmless, these insecurities can actually negatively impact our mental and emotional well-being. They can chip away at our self-esteem, leaving us feeling like we're never good enough. They can create a constant undercurrent of anxiety and self-doubt.

But most importantly, these insecurities can hold us back from fully experiencing the world around us. Imagine wanting to pursue your dream of becoming a fashion designer but feeling held back by worries about your appearance. Or missing out on fun pool parties with friends because you feel self-conscious in a swimsuit. And it's not just about social situations; feeling insecure about your body can even affect your health, like avoiding seeking medical attention because you don't want anyone, even the doctor, to comment on your weight. In fact, research shows that body insecurity can even lead to harmful habits, including disordered eating and self-harming behaviors (*How to Deal*, 2024).

As you can see, these are just some of the ways our insecurities can stop us from living life to the fullest and embracing all the amazing experiences the world has to offer. It's like standing on the sidelines of life, watching opportunities pass by while we're stuck obsessing about how we look.

Where Do Insecurities Come From?

That being said, everybody has insecurities! Some people get insecure from time to time, and some are insecure most of the time. It is a common human experience, and its roots can be traced back to various factors in our lives. Now, think of insecurities like weeds in your garden. Just as different factors contribute to the growth of weeds—such as soil quality, sunlight, and water—various aspects of our lives contribute to feelings of insecurity. And just as weeds come in different shapes and sizes, insecurities manifest in different forms, each affecting us in unique ways.

One reason insecurity can arise is due to recent failures or rejections. According to research, up to 40% of our happiness is influenced by recent life events, with relationship breakups, job loss, and health problems being major contributors (Greenberg, 2015). These experiences can exacerbate feelings of unworthiness, especially for those with pre-existing low self-esteem. For instance, if you've just broken up with a long-term partner, this event can trigger a wave of emotions like sadness, anger, and loneliness, accompanied by feelings of failure and rejection. Your confidence takes a hit, making it challenging to see yourself in a positive light.

Many of us also struggle with confidence in social situations. Past experiences of bullying or exclusion, as well as having critical parents, can contribute to a heightened sensitivity to others' opinions. For instance, imagine someone preparing for a job interview. Memories of being teased or excluded in school due to their appearance, along with critical comments from family members, may heighten their insecurities. This could make them feel self-conscious or doubt their ability to secure the job because they may not fit the perceived image of an ideal candidate. These thoughts might even lead them to choose not to attend the interview altogether.

Lastly, insecurity can come from trying to be perfect all the time. When you're a perfectionist, you might criticize yourself often and feel anxious or not good enough, especially when things don't go as planned. For instance, imagine you're trying to get the perfect body. Even if you exercise and eat well, you might not see the results you want right away. This can make you frustrated and critical of yourself. This relentless pursuit of perfection traps you in a cycle of insecurity and unrealistic expectations, making it challenging to appreciate your progress or pause to consider why this ideal is so important to you in the first place.

The good news is, now that you have a clearer understanding of what's causing your insecurities and how they impact your life, you're in a better position to overcome them! Whether it's dealing with setbacks, managing social anxieties, or battling perfectionism, there are strategies that can help you navigate these feelings and develop a more positive self-image. Through self-awareness, self-compassion, and perseverance, you can break free from insecurity and become more confident.

Nurturing Through Self-Talk

Changing the way we talk to ourselves is a powerful way to overcome insecurities. We briefly touched upon self-talk in the previous chapters, so now let's dive deeper into it! Self-talk refers to the conversations you have with yourself in your mind. When your self-talk is negative, constantly focusing on your flaws or mistakes, it can intensify your insecurities. For instance, if you dislike how you look in a photo, you might immediately think to yourself, *I'm so ugly!* This negative self-talk only makes you feel worse about yourself and your body.

On the other hand, when you talk to yourself positively, it can boost your confidence and even help you handle challenges better. Using the same example, instead of criticizing yourself, your immediate thought might be, *This is how I naturally look when I'm happy, and I'm glad that memory was captured!* This supportive self-talk can help improve your body image because it empowers you to embrace yourself wholeheartedly.

Based on a number of studies, positive self-talk offers many benefits. These include reducing anxiety and obsessive thinking during challenging times, promoting healthier coping mechanisms for emotions and mental stress, enhancing motivation and performance, and boosting self-esteem. Conversely, negative self-talk may lead to a self-fulfilling prophecy. For instance, if you repeatedly tell yourself that you'll never be happy with your body, you may avoid trying new activities or pursuing opportunities that could boost your confidence. As a result, you miss out on potentially fulfilling experiences, reinforcing your negative belief. This pattern of thinking, known as repetitive negative thinking, has been linked to increased severity, persistence, and relapse of body image issues and related emotional distress, such as depression and anxiety (Richards, 2022).

Ways to Practice Positive Self-Talk

Now that you understand the impact of self-talk on your well-being, it's time to rewrite the narrative! Here are some practical strategies you can incorporate into your daily life to pep up that inner dialogue and boost your confidence:

Monitor your inner dialogue: Start by paying attention to your thoughts. Notice when you're being hard on yourself or engaging in negative self-talk. Awareness is the first step to making a change. When you catch yourself thinking negatively, challenge those thoughts. Ask yourself if they're really true or if there's a more positive way to view the situation. For example, if you're thinking, *I look terrible,* challenge that thought by reminding yourself of times when you felt confident and beautiful.

Befriend your inner critic: Instead of seeing that nagging voice in your head as your archenemy, try to welcome it as a misunderstood companion. It's a part of you too, after all! It's that side of you that's trying to keep you safe, albeit in a clumsy way. By befriending your inner critic, you start a conversation rather than a battle. When you get the urge to silence it, try asking "What's really bothering you?" and "Why are you upset?" This approach softens the edges of self-criticism and peels back the layers to uncover the fears and insecurities driving your critical thoughts.

Talk to yourself like a friend: Treat yourself as you would a friend—offer kindness and understanding in both the good and tough times. Rather than dwelling on your mistakes or setbacks, acknowledge them with understanding and forgiveness. Remind yourself that everyone makes mistakes and faces obstacles, and it's okay to not be perfect. Additionally, celebrate your achievements and successes! Allow yourself to bask in the joy of your accomplishments and pat yourself on the back for your efforts and progress.

During challenging times, refer to yourself in the third person: When faced with tough days, try referring to yourself in the third person. It might sound a bit odd at first, but taking this approach creates a little distance from the situation, helping you see things more clearly. For example, if your name is Emma, instead of saying, "I feel insecure about my body," say, "Emma is feeling a bit unsure about her body today." This subtle shift in language can help you detach from intense emotions, reduce self-criticism, and gain a broader perspective on the situation.

Start a gratitude practice: Take a few moments each day to reflect on things you're grateful for. It could be as simple as appreciating a sunny day or a tasty meal. This helps shift your focus from negativity to positivity. When you actively acknowledge the good things in your life, no matter how small, it helps you develop a more optimistic outlook. Instead of dwelling on your insecurities or shortcomings, you train your mind to recognize and appreciate the positive aspects of life. Over time, this habit of gratitude reinforces a mindset of self-affirmation.

Set daily reminders: Setting daily reminders is a practical way to infuse your day with positivity and self-affirmation. Whether it's through sticky notes on your mirror, alerts on your phone, or even setting alarms with encouraging messages, these reminders serve as gentle nudges to practice positive self-talk throughout the day. For instance, your reminder could say, "You are beautiful just the way you are," or "Your worth is not defined by your appearance." By adding these reminders into your daily routine, you create an environment for yourself that reinforces self-love and acceptance.

Make yourself laugh: Making yourself laugh is a powerful tool for combating negative self-talk and boosting your mood. Whether it's watching a funny movie, listening to a comedy podcast, or simply recalling a humorous memory, laughter has the remarkable ability to shift your perspective and uplift your spirits. When you find yourself overwhelmed by insecurities or self-doubt, taking a moment to inject humor into the situation can break the cycle of negative thinking and bring a sense of lightness to your day.

By weaving these strategies into your daily life, you're laying the groundwork for a brighter, more uplifting inner dialogue. Remind yourself that reshaping your self-talk is like planting a garden—it takes time, nurturing, and a lot of patience. Celebrate each tiny victory along the way. You've got this!

Body Confidence 101

Fashion is like a language, and your outfit is the message you send out into the world. Think about it: What do the clothes others wear say about them? Perhaps you notice someone sporting a vintage band tee, signaling their love for music that speaks to their soul. Or maybe you see someone rocking a bold floral print, hinting at their vibrant and free-spirited personality. Each outfit offers a unique glimpse into the individuality and character of the person wearing it.

However, for people who struggle with poor body image, the world of fashion might seem daunting or even inaccessible. When you don't feel confident in your own skin, it can be challenging to embrace clothing as a form of self-expression. The pressure to adhere to certain beauty standards portrayed in the media can make it feel like there's a narrow definition of what is considered fashionable or acceptable. As a result, you might find yourself avoiding certain styles or trends, feeling like they're off-limits because they don't align with your perceived flaws or insecurities.

For instance, you might come across a stunning dress while browsing in a store, but you hesitate to try it on because you're convinced it won't flatter your body shape. Despite feeling drawn to the colors and design, you ultimately decide against it, fearing that it will only accentuate your flaws. Instead, you opt for something safe and familiar, even though it doesn't excite or represent you. This creates a barrier between you and the joy of expressing yourself through fashion.

So, take a moment to reflect: What do your favorite pieces reveal about you? If you don't like the answer, or maybe you're still figuring it out, don't worry! Here are some tips to help you use fashion confidently as a way to showcase your identity:

Get to know yourself: Start by reflecting on your personality, interests, and lifestyle. Consider creating a mood board or Pinterest board to collect images of styles that resonate with you. Pay attention to how certain fabrics, colors, and silhouettes make you feel when you wear them.

Embrace your body: Focus on finding clothing that fits well and flatters your body shape. Invest in pieces that make you feel confident and comfortable. Also, many off-the-rack clothes may not fit perfectly because everyone's body is unique, so don't be afraid to tailor clothing if needed.

Step out of your comfort zone: Start small by incorporating new elements into your outfits, such as experimenting with bold accessories or trying a different color palette. Push yourself to try one new style or trend each season to keep your wardrobe fresh and exciting.

Mix and match: Get creative with your wardrobe by layering different textures, colors, and patterns. Play around with accessories like scarves, hats, and statement jewelry to add personality to your outfits. Don't be afraid to break traditional fashion "rules" and trust your instincts. Fashion is your canvas for self-expression, so seize the opportunity to showcase your unique style!

Seek inspiration: Use fashion influencers and magazines as sources of inspiration but adapt their looks to fit your personal style. Experiment with different aesthetics and trends to find what resonates with you the most.

Confidence is key: Stand tall and carry yourself with confidence in whatever you wear. Remember that confidence is the best accessory, so hold your head high and own your unique style.

Fashion is about enjoyment and expression. Have fun showcasing your personality through clothing. Embrace your unique style and wear what boosts your confidence and happiness, regardless of what others say!

Flaunting Confidence in Public

In the beginning, you might feel like your style is perfectly fine at home or on social media, but when it comes to stepping out in public, you may hesitate, especially when considering wearing what may be referred to as "revealing" clothing. Revealing clothing typically refers to garments that expose more skin or accentuate certain parts of the body. The level of "revealingness" can vary depending on cultural norms, personal preferences, and the context in which the clothing is worn. For example, a crop top or swimsuit might be considered revealing in some cultures, while in others, they are a common and accepted fashion choices, especially during hot summer months. So, what's considered revealing is totally subjective and can differ from person to person.

Therefore, instead of worrying about what others might think, why not seize the opportunity to express yourself authentically? By confidently wearing what makes you feel good, regardless of whether they're deemed "revealing" or not, you assert ownership over your body and style. This act of self-expression can help foster a positive body image and boost self-confidence. When you feel comfortable and confident in your own skin, it radiates outward, empowering you to embrace your whole self and live more fully in the moment.

I understand that this is easier said than done, so here are a few practical suggestions on how to start embracing your style more confidently in public, particularly when it comes to wearing revealing clothing:

Start small: Begin by incorporating small elements of revealing clothing into your outfits, such as a crop top paired with high-waisted pants or a swimsuit worn under a sheer cover-up. This allows you to gradually become comfortable with showing more skin in public.

Find your comfort zone: Experiment with different styles and cuts of revealing clothing to find what makes you feel most comfortable and confident. Whether it's a halter-neck swimsuit or a cropped tank top, choose pieces that align with your personal style and preferences. When you feel physically comfortable, it's easier to feel confident in what you're wearing.

Accessorize: Accessorizing can help enhance your confidence when wearing revealing clothing. Consider adding statement jewelry, a stylish hat, or a trendy pair of sunglasses to complete your look and boost your overall confidence.

Engage in confidence-building exercises: Practice confidence-building exercises, such as standing tall with good posture, making eye contact, and smiling confidently. These small actions can make a big difference in how you perceive yourself and how others perceive you when wearing revealing clothing.

Practice visualization: Visualize yourself confidently wearing revealing clothing in different social situations. Imagine yourself walking with poise and grace, smiling confidently, and owning your unique style. Visualization can help build your confidence and prepare you mentally for wearing revealing clothing in public.

Remember your "why": Reflect on why you want to embrace your style more confidently. Whether it's to express yourself authentically, challenge societal norms, or simply feel good about yourself, keeping your motivations in mind can help fuel your confidence and determination.

Celebrate your progress: Whether it's trying on a new swimsuit or rocking a crop top for the first time, acknowledge your progress, and give yourself a pat on the back for stepping outside of your comfort zone.

This helps you build momentum and encourages you to keep pushing forward, even when faced with challenges or setbacks.

By incorporating these practical suggestions into your daily life, you can gradually build confidence and embrace your style more confidently in public! Remember to prioritize self-love and acceptance, and that it's perfectly fine to take things one step at a time.

Loving Your Postpartum Body

Since we are on the topic of body confidence, it's important to shine a light on a group of women often left out of the conversation: mothers. The journey to body acceptance after childbirth can be a tough one! During the postpartum period, women experience significant physical changes, including weight gain, stretch marks, loose skin, and more. Add to that hormonal roller coasters and the whirlwind of new motherhood—from sleepless nights to round-the-clock care for the baby—and it can really take a toll on one's mood and self-esteem. With so much on their plates, self-care often takes a backseat, leaving many new moms feeling overwhelmed and disconnected from their bodies.

Whether you're a new mom, or maybe it's been a while but you're struggling with confidence after becoming one, this one's for you! Loving and accepting your body becomes even more important after having kids. So, here are a few simple strategies to help you feel more confident in your postpartum body:

Practice self-compassion: Acknowledge the amazing changes your body has gone through to bring new life into the world. You could set aside a few minutes each day for self-reflection and gratitude. Write down three things you appreciate about your body and the amazing journey it has been on. Here are some journaling prompts you could use:

What aspects of my postpartum body do I appreciate or feel proud of?

Are there any specific features of my postpartum body that I struggle to accept or feel insecure about?

What messages about postpartum bodies have I received from society, media, or others around me that I would like to challenge?

In what ways has my body supported me through pregnancy, childbirth, and caring for my baby?

How has my relationship with my body changed since becoming a mom?

Surround yourself with positive people: A strong support system is crucial, especially for new moms. Identify friends and family who uplift and encourage you and prioritize spending time with them. Arrange regular video calls or meetups whenever you need a reminder that you are strong, beautiful, and loved unconditionally.

Curate a postpartum wardrobe: Select outfits that fit well and boost your confidence. Invest in a few staple pieces that complement your postpartum body. Embrace new styles that highlight your favorite features. And if any pre-birth clothes don't spark joy, consider setting them aside. Surround yourself with clothing that empowers you and makes you feel fantastic!

Start each day with mindful intention: Before starting your day, look in the mirror and say one thing you want to focus on to improve your relationship with your body. For example, "Today, I will nourish my body with healthy and delicious meals, ensuring I have the energy to take care of myself and my baby." You could also add some positive affirmations. Here are a few you could use:

I embrace my postpartum body with love and acceptance, knowing that it has given me the greatest gift of all.

I trust in my body's innate wisdom to heal and restore itself.

I am grateful for the miraculous journey my body has undertaken to bring new life into this world.

I embrace my body's journey through motherhood.

I appreciate all that my body has done and continues to do for me and my baby.

I release any negative thoughts about my postpartum body and choose to honor its unique beauty.

Take time for self-care: Indulge in self-care activities that leave you feeling renewed and revitalized. Whether it's unwinding with a soothing bath, strolling in nature, or engaging in a hobby, carve out a precious 15 minutes each day just for yourself.

Be mindful of your media intake: In the whirlwind of new motherhood, it's important to keep an eye on what messages you are consuming. While platforms like Instagram and Facebook can be supportive, they can also flood you with unrealistic standards of postpartum bodies. Customize your social media feed to include accounts that celebrate real postpartum bodies and motherhood journeys. Prioritize real-life connections with friends and family. Remind yourself that your worth is not determined by how closely you resemble the images you see in the media.

Seek professional support if needed: Don't hesitate to reach out to a therapist or counselor who can provide guidance and support. These professionals can offer valuable guidance and support to help you navigate the challenges and rediscover your confidence and self-worth. You don't have to do it all on your own.

Remember, every body is different, and it's normal for your postpartum body to undergo changes as it heals and adjusts to motherhood. But one thing is certain: You deserve to feel confident and empowered in your postpartum body!

Uplifting Others

When you are confident in your body, you radiate positivity and inspire those around you to embrace their own unique beauty as well. Think about it: Were there ever people who made you think, *I want to be that comfortable in myself,* or something similar? Well, you could be one of those people, too! Your efforts toward self-acceptance can have a ripple effect, creating a supportive environment where everyone feels accepted and celebrated in their own skin. So, let's talk about some of the ways you can spread love and uplift others in their body positivity journey.

First, lead by example. Show others that confidence is about embracing imperfections and celebrating individuality. For example, you could encourage others to join you in activities that promote self-care or remind them of their positive traits when they're talking negatively about the way they look.

Another simple way is to compliment others beyond their looks. A genuine compliment can brighten someone's day and boost their confidence. So, acknowledge others for their talents, strengths, and achievements rather than just their appearance. You might praise a friend for their creativity, kindness, or resilience in overcoming challenges. If it's someone you just met, focus on something that reflects their effort, like their style. By shifting the focus away from their body, you're not only making someone feel appreciated but also reinforcing the idea that true beauty comes from within.

You could also uplift others by standing firm on what you won't tolerate. For instance, refuse to engage in conversations that perpetuate body shaming or unrealistic beauty standards. If you find yourself in such a situation, you could redirect the conversation in a calm and empathetic manner. You might say something like, "I've been trying to be more mindful about the way I talk about bodies. Let's chat about [insert different topic] instead!"

If the person you're conversing with gets offended, encourage open dialogue and let them know that you're willing to listen to their perspective as well. This is actually another effective way to uplift others. Bodies are not shameful; we all have them, yet discussions about them can often become heated. So, offer a listening ear and a supportive presence to those who may be struggling with their body image. Provide empathy and understanding. Keep in mind that everyone is on their own timeline in this journey, and that your words have the power to shape perceptions and attitudes.

Lastly, when you encounter body-shaming comments or unrealistic beauty standards, instead of remaining silent, address the issue directly by expressing your disagreement. Emphasize the importance of embracing all body types and celebrating individuality. Additionally, encourage others to join you in promoting a more inclusive mindset by sharing positive messages and examples of diverse beauty. By actively advocating for change, you contribute to a culture that values and respects people of all shapes, sizes, and backgrounds.

***

Now that you've bravely tackled your insecurities and championed confidence in yourself and others, it's time to shift your focus to nurturing your body! In the next chapter, we'll dive into the role of nutrition in fueling your overall well-being and healing your connection with your body.

Know Your Body

Weight loss does not make people happy. Or peaceful. Being thin does not address the emptiness that has no shape or weight or name. Even a wildly successful diet is a colossal failure because inside the new body is the same sinking heart. -Geneen Roth

In a piece for Women's Health magazine, writer Jamie Mendell opens up about her journey toward health and happiness. Jamie first got into a diet at age 17. Despite being perfectly healthy, she knew her teenage body was changing, and that fact scared her. So, she controlled what she ate, and soon enough, without her realizing, she was tying her self-worth to her weight and appearance.

"Up until that point, I had prided myself on having a skinny, athletic body, and without that, I wasn't sure what I had to offer," Jamie shared (para. 1).

That initial diet stretched out over a decade, a constant cycle of restriction followed by uncontrollable eating. Even as she succeeded in other areas of her life, she carried a secret shame about her binge eating. Her "battle" with food and the rollercoaster of weight fluctuations left Jamie feeling emotionally drained. Despite her many achievements, Jamie struggled to understand why she couldn't conquer her relationship with food.

"I had spent 10 years absolutely consumed with thoughts about food. My life was dull, and I felt trapped in an endless cycle," she wrote (para. 3).

However, as Jamie approached her 26th birthday, she felt a sudden shift within herself. The ticking clock and a sense of urgency nudged her to reassess her approach to life. It dawned on her that her insecurities surrounding her body were holding her back from fully embracing experiences, like dinners with friends and dating. This realization was a game-changer! Jamie made a choice: to bid farewell to dieting.

She then embarked on a journey of self-discovery and self-care, embracing life fully by focusing on her relationships, pursuing her passions, and prioritizing her emotional and physical well-being. She finally learned to let go of societal pressures and expectations, choosing happiness and self-acceptance over the number on the scale.

As Jamie continued to create a life she loved, she found that her reliance on food was actually a coping mechanism that gradually diminished the happier she became. Over time, her weight naturally settled at its most comfortable range. But, more importantly, Jamie realized that her worth was not dependent on her size.

"I learned who I was outside of food and my body. I discovered new passions, what lit me up, and what made me happy. I met myself again," Jamie concluded (Mendell, 2015, para. 20).

From a young age, many of us unwittingly become part of a widespread cultural trend: diet culture. This culture, focused on restricting food and dissatisfaction with our bodies, seeps into every aspect of our lives subtly. Talks about weight loss are inescapable. They permeate magazine articles, social media posts, television commercials, advertisements, and more. Everywhere we turn, there seems to be a new fad diet, detox program, or "miracle" weight loss solution promising quick results and the perfect body. What's worse is they often glamorize extreme measures such as restrictive eating, excessive exercise, and the use of diet pills or unregulated supplements.

Even well-intended advice from family or professionals often reinforces the idea that being thin equates to being healthy and, therefore, happy. Over time, diet culture becomes ingrained in us, shaping our beliefs about food, beauty, health, and our own worth. The underlying message is clear: We must constantly strive to shrink ourselves in order to be worthy of love, acceptance, and success.

What we're rarely taught is how to listen to our bodies and trust our own judgment. Since we are encouraged to follow strict rules and guidelines imposed by external sources, we often lose touch with our own internal wisdom when it comes to nourishing ourselves. That's why many of us embark on a journey to mend not only our relationship with our bodies but also with its main fuel: food.

The Importance of Nutrition

Diet culture bombards us with messages that equate healthy eating solely with weight loss. That is why, while we all understand that nutrition is important, many of us have distorted perceptions of what it truly means to eat healthily.

Healthy eating goes far beyond the number on the scale. It's about nourishing our bodies with foods that support our overall well-being. Good nutrition simply means that your body is receiving the essential nutrients, vitamins, and minerals necessary for it to function at its best. Proper nutrition is important because it has been proven to help prevent diseases like heart disease, diabetes, stroke, and some cancers. It also helps lower high blood pressure and cholesterol levels, improves overall well-being, strengthens the body's ability to fight off illness, aids in recovery from illness or injury, and boosts energy levels (*The Importance of Good Nutrition*, 2023).

According to the World Health Organization (2020), a balanced diet varies based on factors such as age, gender, lifestyle, physical activity level, cultural context, available foods, and dietary customs. This means that there isn't a one-size-fits-all approach to eating healthy. So, those trendy meal plans you see in magazines or on social media might not be appropriate for everyone.

How Food Affects Body Image

The intersection between food and body image is complex. Our relationship with food is deeply intertwined with how we perceive our bodies, and vice versa. In a society where slimness is often praised as the epitome of beauty, many of us develop misconceptions about food. Let's take a closer look at some of the most common ones.

Myth #1: Dieting Teaches Discipline

Many people perceive dieting as a means of disciplining the mind and body. However, in reality, unless recommended by a nutritionist, self-imposed dieting often only promotes unhealthy behaviors and attitudes toward food.

Let's dive into the life cycle of a restrictive diet for a minute. It typically begins with enthusiasm and determination, as you commit to adhering to strict guidelines dictating what, when, and how much you should eat. This initial phase can bring about a sense of control and accomplishment, especially as you may notice short-term weight loss or changes in your body shape, reinforcing the belief that the diet is working.

However, as time passes, the initial excitement fades, giving way to feelings of deprivation. Your body starts to react to the restricted intake, both physically and mentally. Metabolism slows down, hunger intensifies, and thoughts of food consume your mind.

Eventually, the strict rules of the diet become unsustainable. Despite your best efforts to adhere to them, you often find yourself breaking them more frequently. This breach of the diet's guidelines often triggers emotions like guilt and anxiety around eating. If you've ever been on a diet, you're probably familiar with the feeling of self-loathing that comes from "giving in" to a slice of cake.

Instead of teaching discipline, restrictive diets foster negative self-talk, as participants blame themselves for their lack of willpower when, in fact, 95% of diets don't work because they set our bodies up for failure (Hungate, 2021). We naturally crave food because we need it to live. Denying ourselves food when we're hungry is not something the human body is designed to sustain in the long run.

Myth #2: Carbs Are Bad

Carbohydrates, or carbs, are one of the three macronutrients essential for providing energy to the body, alongside fats and proteins. They serve as the primary source of fuel for the brain and muscles, playing a crucial role in supporting both physical and cognitive function.

The misconception that carbs are unhealthy often stems from the belief that refined carbohydrates, such as white bread, sugary snacks, and pastries, lead to significant weight gain. While it's true that not all carbs are created equal, and whole, unprocessed carbohydrates—such as whole grains, fruits, and vegetables—may be healthier for the body in the long run, a comprehensive study found no significant disparities between the two in terms of weight management (Leech, 2024).

So, it's a good idea to think about foods as a whole rather than fixating solely on their nutrient composition. Choose options that are satisfying to you and your body. When it comes to carbs specifically, they can be included as part of a balanced diet and need not be avoided altogether.

Myth #3: There Are "Good" and "Bad" Foods

The concept of categorizing foods as either "good" or "bad" is deeply ingrained in our society. Foods commonly labeled as "bad" tend to be those high in sugar, fat, or calories, while "good" foods are often perceived as being low in these nutrients and high in vitamins, minerals, and fiber.

However, in reality, no single food is inherently good or bad; instead, a balanced diet is defined by variety and moderation rather than strict categorizations. Having fast food, for example, is not a sin, and eating only vegetables every day is not necessarily virtuous. Labeling foods as "good" or "bad" only fosters feelings of guilt or shame around eating, which can contribute to an unhealthy relationship with food.

Instead of categorizing foods in terms of morality, it's more helpful to approach nutrition with a balanced and inclusive mindset. All foods, including ice cream and soda, can be part of a healthy diet if consumed in moderation and as part of a varied eating pattern. Unless it's for a specific medical or cultural reason, any food that nourishes you and brings you joy is beneficial for you.

Myth #4: A Detox Diet Will Rid Your Body of Toxins

Detox diets typically involve restrictive eating patterns, such as consuming only fruit juices, smoothies, or raw vegetables, while eliminating processed foods, caffeine, alcohol, and other substances deemed "toxic." Some also incorporate supplements, herbal teas, or colon cleanses claiming to enhance the body's detoxification processes.

However, your body already has natural detox processes, like your liver and kidneys, which work continuously to remove toxins. While environmental pollutants do pose health risks and can accumulate in the body over time, detox diets offer little to no evidence-based strategies for addressing these concerns. In fact, what they consider as "toxins" is often vague, and the mechanisms of how the detox works are usually unclear.

Overall, research shows that there is little to no evidence that detox diets help remove any toxins from your body (Bjarnadottir, 2023). Instead of relying on them, you can support your body's natural detoxification processes by adopting a balanced and nutritious diet.

Myth #5: Skipping Meals Helps With Weight Loss

Many people believe that skipping meals, especially when you've eaten more than usual the meal before, can significantly reduce their calorie intake, leading to weight loss. However, this approach usually backfires and can have negative effects on overall health.

Research shows that skipping meals might cause you to overeat later and can even slow down your metabolism, as your body tries to conserve energy in response to the perceived food scarcity. This can make weight management even more challenging. Furthermore, skipping meals can disrupt your body's natural hunger and fullness cues, which can contribute to disordered eating behaviors and an unhealthy relationship with food. Instead, focus on eating balanced meals and snacks to fuel your body efficiently throughout the day (Kuppersmith & Kennedy, 2005).

As you can see, these misconceptions often lead to unrealistic expectations about what constitutes a healthy diet and fuel harmful behaviors related to food and body image. By moving away from a diet culture mindset, we can develop a healthier relationship with food and our bodies.

The Prevalence of Disordered Eating

With so many misconceptions about food and nutrition, it's no surprise that disordered eating is widespread. In fact, a survey revealed that approximately two-thirds of American women aged 25 to 45 reported having disordered eating patterns (University of North Carolina at Chapel Hill, 2008). This might seem surprising, especially if you believe that disordered eating only applies to those diagnosed with an eating disorder, such as anorexia or bulimia. However, that's not entirely the case. Disordered eating, while definitely different from diagnosed disorders, can still negatively affect your well-being. Let's take a closer look at the distinction between the two.

Disordered eating refers to unhealthy eating patterns and attitudes toward food that don't meet the criteria for an eating disorder but can still harm health. While not as severe as diagnosed eating disorders, unaddressed disordered eating may lead to their development. Your eating habits might be disordered if you engage in the following behaviors:

Extreme healthy eating: You might cut out all carbs because you think they're bad for you.

Avoiding certain foods: You might skip foods with gluten, even if you don't have a diagnosed gluten intolerance.

Binge eating: You eat a lot of food quickly, even if it makes you feel sick.

Labeling foods: You only eat what you consider "good" foods and avoid anything you think is "bad."

Emotional eating: You snack when you're stressed or bored to deal with your feelings.

Extreme dieting or exercise: You follow strict diets or intense workout routines that might harm your health.

Food rituals: You have specific routines before eating, like arranging your food in a certain way.

Skipping meals: You regularly skip meals, either because you're busy or want to eat less.

Purging: You make yourself throw up after eating to control your weight or deal with guilt.

Misusing pills: You take diuretics or laxatives often to try to lose weight or "cleanse" your body.

Engaging in these behaviors can disrupt your relationship with food and body image, causing not only potential health issues, but also emotional distress (Fuller, 2022a).

On the other hand, an eating disorder is a diagnosed mental health condition in which individuals engage in the above-mentioned behaviors, but to a more severe extent, usually driven by intense anxiety and preoccupation with food and body image.

There are many types of eating disorders, with the most common one being anorexia nervosa, which is marked by an intense fear of gaining weight. Those with anorexia often perceive themselves as overweight, even when they are significantly underweight in reality. Symptoms of anorexia nervosa include extreme weight loss, an obsession with counting calories, meticulously monitoring food intake, denial of hunger, a distorted body image, social withdrawal, fatigue, weakness, thin or brittle hair and nails, cold intolerance, irregular menstrual periods, and the development of fine body hair, known as lanugo, as the body attempts to stay warm.

The negative effects of anorexia nervosa can be severe and far-reaching. Physically, it can lead to serious complications such as malnutrition, dehydration, electrolyte imbalances, heart problems, kidney failure, and even death. Psychologically, individuals with anorexia may experience depression, anxiety, social isolation, and suicidal thoughts (Petre, 2022). Anorexia nervosa is considered one of the deadliest mental disorders (Gutman-Wei, 2023).

If you recognize symptoms of an eating disorder or disordered eating in yourself, don't hesitate to reach out to a healthcare professional. They can provide valuable guidance and resources to support you. Remember, you're not alone in this, and seeking help is the first step toward recovery.

Repairing Your Relationship With Food

If you find yourself viewing food in a negative light, you're not alone. Many of us have been conditioned by diet culture to see certain foods as "good" or "bad," leading to guilt and anxiety around eating. It's important to remind ourselves that food is not the enemy!

Here are some tips on how you can shift your perspective and foster a more positive relationship with food:

Listen to your body's hunger and fullness cues: When you're hungry, your body may communicate this through physical sensations like stomach growling, feelings of emptiness, or a lack of energy. On the other hand, signs of fullness may include a feeling of satisfaction, a decrease in hunger pangs, or simply no longer feeling the urge to eat. Pay attention to these cues. Eat when you're hungry and stop when you're satisfied. This promotes a more intuitive approach to eating, cultivating trust with your body and ultimately strengthening your relationship with both food and yourself, removing the need for external guidelines.

Avoid labeling foods: When you label foods as "good" or "bad," you introduce a sense of moral judgment around eating, which can lead to feelings of guilt or shame. Instead of categorizing foods as "off-limits" or "forbidden," try using more neutral or positive language. For example, rather than saying, "I shouldn't eat this cake slice," you could say, "I choose to enjoy cake occasionally as part of a balanced diet." This shift in language empowers you to make conscious choices without imposing unnecessary restrictions or judgments on certain foods. As previously discussed, a balanced diet emphasizes moderation and balance, rather than strict rules or deprivation.

Practice mindful eating: Mindful eating means being present in the moment and engaging all your senses while eating. It involves avoiding distractions like screens or multitasking so you can savor each bite. This approach encourages you to eat more slowly and pay attention to how different foods make you feel. By practicing mindfulness, you can develop a deeper appreciation for food, enhance your relationship with eating, and make more informed choices about nourishing your body. To get started, try answering some of these questions during meal times or journal about them afterward:

How does the food taste? Pay attention to the flavors as you chew slowly.

How satisfied are you feeling as you eat? Check in with your hunger and fullness cues throughout the meal.

Are you eating because you're hungry, or is it for other reasons? Tune into your body's signals to distinguish between physical hunger and emotional cravings.

What emotions are you experiencing while eating? Notice any feelings of pleasure, guilt, or discomfort associated with the food.

How does your body feel after eating? Pay attention to how different foods affect your energy levels and overall well-being.

Give yourself permission to eat: Giving yourself permission to eat involves liberating yourself from restrictive rules or guilt and embracing the enjoyment of eating without judgment. It's about realizing that all foods can have a place in a balanced diet. When you find yourself thinking, "I shouldn't..." when wanting to eat something, recognize that it's okay to indulge occasionally and that one meal or snack doesn't define your overall health. Instead, say "My body deserves nourishment," or "I am allowed to enjoy this without guilt."

Learn more about nutrition from reputable sources: Start by familiarizing yourself with the basic principles of nutrition, such as the importance of consuming a variety of fruits, vegetables, whole grains, lean proteins, and healthy fats. Additionally, learn to discern reliable sources. Be cautious of exaggerated promises or claims of quick fixes, miracle cures, or "secret" ingredients. By becoming more knowledgeable about nutrition, you can feel more confident in the food choices you make.

By incorporating these strategies into your daily life, you can gradually shift your mindset and develop a healthier relationship with food, free from judgment and restriction. Remember that food is meant to be enjoyed and nourish your body, not to cause guilt or shame. Be patient and kind to yourself every step of the way.

Finding Joy in Movement

Nutrition and exercise are inseparable components of a healthy lifestyle, each playing a distinct role in supporting overall well-being. Nutrition is like the fuel that powers your body, providing energy and essential nutrients. Exercise then uses this energy efficiently, keeping your body healthy. They work together like a well-oiled machine, ensuring you move and feel your best. That's why we can't talk about nutrition without discussing physical movement too.

Diet culture has also significantly shaped how we view exercise, often portraying it as a tool primarily for losing weight or changing our bodies. Think about it: We see countless advertisements promoting exercise programs with promises of "getting a bikini body" or "melting away fat." Fitness influencers or celebrity coaches often place heavy emphasis on their toned bodies, implying that achieving such a physique is the ultimate goal of exercise. Even workout routines shared in magazines or online articles tend to focus on calorie burning and achieving a certain aesthetic rather than promoting overall health and well-being. As a result, many people view exercise as a means to an end, rather than an enjoyable activity that contributes to their overall health.

The truth is, regular exercise offers a myriad of benefits that extend beyond aesthetics. These include a longer lifespan, stronger bones, enhanced mobility, and a reduced risk of many health conditions such as heart disease, hypertension, diabetes, and colon cancer. Additionally, exercise improves mental well-being by alleviating symptoms of anxiety and depression (Illinois Department of Public Health, n.d.).

According to the American Heart Association (2021), a good rule of thumb is to aim for at least 150 minutes of moderate-intensity aerobic activity or 75 minutes of high-intensity aerobic activity per week. Moderate-intensity aerobic activity refers to physical activities that increase your heart rate and breathing but still allow you to carry on a conversation, such as walking or cycling at a moderate pace. High-intensity aerobic activity, on the other hand, is more intense and will cause your heart rate and breathing to increase significantly, making it challenging to carry on a conversation. Examples include running, swimming laps, and playing basketball.

You can schedule your exercise in one go or break it up into 10 to 20-minute daily intervals. If you lead a sedentary lifestyle, meaning you spend most of the day sitting at your desk, any level of activity is beneficial. Even light-intensity exercise can help counteract the negative health effects of prolonged sitting.

How to Actually Enjoy Exercise

Research suggests that people tend to make a habit of activities that bring them pleasure while avoiding those that they associate with pain or discomfort. This is called Hedonic Motivation, and when it comes to exercise, it means that you are more likely to keep up with it if you actually enjoy it (*Want to Exercise More?*, 2017). With that in mind, here are some tips on how to make physical movement something you genuinely look forward to:

Find activities you enjoy: Explore a variety of physical activities to discover what genuinely excites you. Think about activities you naturally enjoy or hobbies you are already passionate about. Whether it's dancing, hiking, swimming, or playing sports, pay attention to how each activity makes you feel physically and emotionally, and select those that leave you energized and fulfilled. Don't hesitate to try new things and step out of your comfort zone! Remember, exercise is any physical movement; it doesn't have to be limited to sports or going to the gym.

Make it social: When you exercise with friends, family, or join classes, it transforms the experience into a shared adventure. Not only does it make the workout more enjoyable, but it also provides opportunities for bonding and connection. Having a workout buddy or being part of a fitness group offers built-in accountability, as you're more likely to stick to your exercise routine when others are relying on you. Overall, exercising with others not only boosts your physical health but also nurtures your social well-being, making it a win-win situation!

Set realistic goals: Set goals that align with your interests and abilities. Begin by identifying what you want to achieve and break it down into smaller, manageable milestones. Whether it's running a certain distance, lifting a specific weight, or mastering a new yoga pose, breaking larger goals into smaller steps makes them less daunting and easier to track. Celebrate each milestone you reach and adjust your goals as needed along the way to keep yourself feeling challenged and motivated.

Schedule it: Treat physical activity as an essential part of your daily routine by scheduling it into your day. Choose specific times when you're most energized and motivated to exercise. By blocking out dedicated time for physical movement in your calendar, you're more likely to follow through and make it happen.

Stage your environment: Creating a positive environment for your workouts can make a significant difference in your experience. Surround yourself with motivational cues that inspire and uplift you, whether it's by curating a playlist of energizing music, displaying motivational quotes in your workout space, or exercising in a beautiful outdoor setting surrounded by nature's beauty. These cues can help shift your mindset and elevate your mood, making exercise feel more enjoyable and rewarding.

Mix it up: Keep your routine fresh and exciting by incorporating a diverse range of exercises and activities. Experiment with new workouts, equipment, or classes to challenge your body in different ways. You could also simply switch up your surroundings. Additionally, inject elements of fun and playfulness into your routine to make exercise feel less like a chore. Try gamifying your workouts by setting challenges or competing with friends. Doing so adds an element of excitement and friendly competition to your physical activity that can prevent boredom from setting in.

Reward yourself: Create a rewards system to celebrate your progress and achievements. Treat yourself to something you enjoy, whether it's a meal, a massage, or a new outfit. These rewards serve as incentives that not only acknowledge your hard work but also provide a sense of satisfaction. By incorporating rewards into your fitness routine, you create a cycle of positivity and motivation that fuels your continued progress and success.

Remember to always listen to your body. Pay attention to its cues and adjust your routine accordingly to ensure a safe and enjoyable experience. By incorporating these strategies, you'll not only nurture a lifelong love for movement but also improve your relationship with your body!

The Role of Rest and Relaxation

Now that we've discussed how important nutrition and physical activity are for your body, it's time to shine a light on another aspect that is just as crucial but often overlooked: making sure you get proper rest and relaxation. Think about it, when was the last time you cleared your schedule to simply do what you wanted or to do nothing at all?

Similar to food, taking time to rest and relax is not something you need to earn. Just as you need nourishment to fuel yourself, you also need rest to recharge your mind and body. Ignoring this need can lead to burnout, decreased productivity, and various health issues. Additionally, without rest days, the benefits you get from physical activity may be nullified because your body is not getting the chance to repair muscles, joints, and other important structures (Fletcher, 2021).

Unfortunately, in this day and age, stress is unavoidable. Over 75% of Americans reported experiencing symptoms of stress, such as headaches, fatigue, or sleep disturbances. Furthermore, 49%, acknowledged that stress has negatively impacted their behavior (SingleCare Team, 2024). While not classified as a disease itself, chronic stress can have detrimental effects on our health and overall quality of life. Moreover, stress can influence our perception of ourselves, affecting body image and self-esteem. Therefore, prioritizing rest and relaxation is not a luxury but a fundamental necessity for maintaining both physical and mental well-being.

How to Rest and Relax the Body

Sleep and stress are closely linked. Stress can disrupt our ability to get good-quality sleep; conversely, inadequate or poor-quality sleep can increase stress levels, creating a vicious cycle. So, it's important to ensure you get a good night's sleep each night. Aim for seven to nine hours of uninterrupted sleep to allow your body and mind to recharge fully (Johnson, 2018). Create a relaxing bedtime routine, such as dimming the lights, taking a warm bath, or practicing relaxation techniques to promote better sleep.

Once you have sleep covered, it's also important to take breaks and recharge throughout the day. Rest can look different to different people, but essentially, it's any activity that helps your body or mind feel rejuvenated. It could involve being active, like going for a walk, or staying passive, like taking a few minutes to sit quietly and breathe deeply. With that in mind, let's explore a few stress-relief strategies you can easily incorporate into your daily routine.

Breathing Exercises

Research shows that breathing exercises can uplift mood, clear thinking, and reduce feelings of stress, anxiety, and depression. Furthermore, studies determined that our brain links different emotions with specific breathing patterns. For instance, when we're happy, our breathing is steady, but when stressed, it becomes irregular and shallow. By engaging in breathing exercises, we can trick our brain into believing we're in a calm state, even during stressful times (Mental Health First Aid USA, 2021).

There are various types of breathing exercises available, but here's a quick and easy one you can try called "box breathing":

Sit comfortably and close your eyes.

Inhale deeply through your nose for a count of four.

Hold your breath for four counts.

Exhale slowly through your mouth for four counts.

Hold your breath again for four counts.

Repeat this process, inhaling, holding, exhaling, and holding again for four counts each time (Ankrom, 2024).

Progressive Muscle Relaxation

Progressive Muscle Relaxation (PMR) is a relaxation technique that involves tensing and then relaxing specific muscle groups in a systematic manner. PMR helps reduce physical stress, which in turn can lead to mental relaxation. When we experience stress or anxiety, our muscles tend to tense up involuntarily as part of the body's fight–or–flight response. By consciously tensing and relaxing the muscles during PMR, we can override this stress response and induce a state of calmness (Nunez, 2020a).

Additionally, PMR can help increase body awareness and mindfulness, allowing us to better recognize and manage stress triggers in our daily lives, as well as develop a stronger relationship with our bodies. Here's how it works:

Find a comfortable spot to sit or lie down.

Take five deep breaths to relax.

Start with your feet. Tighten your toes, hold, then relax.

Move to your calf muscles. Tighten, hold, then relax.

Work your way up, tensing and relaxing each muscle group: knees, thighs, hands, arms, buttocks, and abdomen.

Tighten your chest, hold briefly, then relax as you exhale.

Lift your shoulders, hold, then relax them.

Purse your lips, hold, then relax.

Open your mouth wide, hold, then relax.

Close your eyes tightly, hold, then relax.

Lift your eyebrows, hold, then relax.

Repeat this process as needed to help release tension in the body. Remember to take a moment to breathe deeply and bask in the feeling of relaxation before concluding each exercise.

Guided Imagery

Guided imagery is a relaxation technique that involves using the power of imagination to create calming mental images or scenarios. The process typically involves focusing your attention on specific sensory details, such as sights, sounds, smells, and textures, to create a rich and immersive mental experience. By immersing yourself in calming scenarios, you can temporarily escape from your stressors and experience a sense of mental and emotional relief.

Similar to breathing exercises, there are various guided imagery techniques out there. Here's a simple yet effective one you can try:

Find a quiet and comfortable area to sit or lie down.

Close your eyes. Inhale deeply, exhale slowly, and continue breathing deeply throughout the relaxation exercise.

Imagine yourself sitting on a secluded beach at sunset. Picture the golden hues of the setting sun casting a warm glow across the sky and shimmering on the surface of the calm ocean.

Focus on the details of the scene. Hear the gentle lapping of the waves against the shore, feel the soft, warm sand beneath your feet, and smell the salty sea breeze.

Envision a wooden pathway leading from the shore into a lush, green jungle behind you. Visualize yourself walking along this pathway, surrounded by towering palm trees and vibrant tropical foliage.

Spend several minutes in this mental landscape. Allow yourself to relax fully into the scene.

After approximately 15 minutes, return gently to the present moment by slowly counting to three and opening your eyes.

Repeat this guided imagery exercise regularly to cultivate a sense of inner calm. You can access a variety of guided imagery audio recordings on platforms like YouTube or through apps like Headspace (Nunez, 2020b).

These techniques can easily be incorporated into your daily routine to aid in rest and relaxation. However, you don't have to engage in all of them regularly; simply choose the ones that work best for you!

***

Now that you've learned how to better care for your body through proper nutrition, movement, and stress management, it's time to shift your mindset from chasing appearances to celebrating functionality! Get ready to embrace a new perspective on body image—one that prioritizes feeling strong, capable, and vibrant over looking a certain way.

Lean on Function,
Not Aesthetic

We can't hate ourselves into a version of ourselves we can love. -Lori Deschene

Despite being one of the best tennis players of all time, with an impressive record of 20 Grand Slam titles, Serena Williams has had her fair share of body image struggles. In an interview with HuffPost, Serena opened up about how growing up in the public eye and being constantly compared to her sister, Venus, who is also a tennis star, made her insecure about her body. Venus was the one always praised as beautiful, with her body seen as ideal, while Serena felt hers was too muscular.

"Venus was like a model. I was thicker. Most women athletes are pretty thin. I didn't really know how to deal with it," Serena explained (Bronner, 2015, para. 3).

Like most women, Serena found it difficult to accept and love her body as it is for many years. However, her perspective drastically changed when she sustained a foot injury in 2010. This injury led to two surgeries and a blood clot in her lungs, which almost killed her. Thankfully, she got to the hospital in time after experiencing breathing problems. Still, she was in and out of the hospital and had to stay off the court for months.

"It's like a heartbreak. You worry every second about it," Serena shared (para. 10).

Through the gradual and arduous recovery process, Serena developed a deeper appreciation for her body's strength and resilience. This transformed her outlook not just on her relationship with her body but with life as well.

"Every day I got a little bit stronger. It gave me a new perspective on my life. I realized there are so many things that are so important," Serena concluded (para. 11).

Beauty in Function

It is said that familiarity breeds contempt, and nowhere is this more evident than in our relationship with our own bodies. Day in and day out, we rely on our bodies to carry us through life's challenges and joys, often without a second thought. Yet, in our familiarity, we often overlook the incredible complexity and functionality of the human body, taking for granted the various ways in which it enables us to experience the world around us.

Every movement, every sensation, and every interaction with our environment is made possible by the intricate coordination of our muscles, bones, nerves, and sensory organs. From the beating of our hearts to the firing of neurons in our brains, our bodies are constantly at work, performing a variety of functions that sustain life and enrich our existence. Consider walking, for example. It's thanks to the 26 small yet strong bones in our feet that we're able to accomplish this simple yet remarkable act (Healthline Editorial Team, 2018).

Furthermore, our bodies possess an astonishing capacity for adaptation and resilience in the face of adversity. Whether recovering from injury, illness, or trauma, the human body has an innate ability to heal and regenerate. In fact, every day, each cell in your body experiences tens of thousands of lesions. This continuous damage has the potential to alter a cell's DNA and prompt it to harm body tissue. Fortunately, your body diligently inspects DNA strands and instinctively replaces any damaged parts (Pemberton, 2020).

Beyond the realm of physical function, our bodies also play a crucial role in shaping our identities and connecting us to others. Through gestures, expressions, and nonverbal communication, we express our emotions, thoughts, and intentions, forging bonds with those around us. Indeed, our bodies serve as the canvas upon which we paint the story of our lives! It only takes a gentle reminder for us to realize how marvelous our bodies are and how much they do for us, asking only for compassion and care in return.

The Myth of Aesthetic

Certain bodies are often considered more aesthetically pleasing due to factors such as symmetry, proportion, and adherence to beauty standards. However, as you've previously learned, beauty ideals are subjective and can vary widely across different cultures and time periods. What one person finds attractive, another may not, and vice versa.

In reality, many features commonly perceived as "flaws" are entirely normal and natural variations of the human body. One example is cellulite, which is characterized by the dimpled appearance of the skin, particularly on the thighs and buttocks. Cellulite is a common occurrence that affects individuals of all body types, regardless of weight or fitness level. Despite being stigmatized in popular culture, cellulite is completely normal and does not indicate poor health. In fact, research shows that up to 90% of women will encounter cellulite in their bodies at some point in their lives (Crosta, 2023).

Another common perceived flaw that is actually not is freckles. Freckles are small patches of skin that contain a higher concentration of melanin, the pigment responsible for skin color. They often appear on areas of the body that are exposed to sunlight, such as the face, arms, and shoulders. The development of freckles is influenced by both genetic and environmental factors (Connor, 2023). While beauty standards may lead some people to view freckles as imperfections, they are simply a natural response to sun exposure. In fact, many people, including myself, find them extremely charming.

Scars are also often perceived as flaws, but I believe they should be celebrated more. They serve as visible markers of the body's remarkable ability to heal itself after injury or surgery. While it's true that they may alter the skin's appearance, scars are evidence of our resilience and survival. Each scar tells its own story, whether from a childhood mishap, a surgical procedure, or a significant life event. They are visible reminders of the inherent strength and tenacity within us!

These are just a few examples of what we were made to think were flaws, but they actually highlight the diversity of the human body and emphasize that beauty comes in many forms. These differences illustrate that there is no such thing as a "bad'" body, only negative perceptions of it stemming from societal beauty standards that promote unrealistic ideals. By celebrating these natural variations and reframing them as unique attributes, we can cultivate a greater sense of self-acceptance and appreciation for our bodies, as well as for others'.

The Importance of Loving Your Body for What It Does

As children, we—both girls and boys—were often fascinated by what our bodies could do. We marveled at how high we could jump, how fast we could run, or even if we could manage a backflip on the playground. At this stage, our focus was on the capabilities and functions of our bodies rather than their appearance.

However, as we grew older, we were bombarded with messages from media, advertising, and social norms that dictated what the "ideal" body should look like. We were taught to strive for a certain body shape, size, and appearance. As previously discussed, this emphasis on appearance over function led to a disconnect between ourselves and our bodies, resulting in poor body image and low self-esteem. That's why it was important to reverse what we had been incorrectly taught and return to the mindset we had as children—back when we understood that our bodies were much more than just objects to be looked at.

Research has found that when women perceive their bodies in terms of functionality, they tend to express higher levels of satisfaction and appreciation for their bodies. Additionally, they report feeling more empowered and physically capable (Abbott, 2012). This may be because appreciating our bodies for their functionality leads us to take better care of ourselves and be more open to new experiences.

Simple Body Gratitude Practices

Now, how do you actually love your body for what it can do rather than how it looks? Well, it all starts with gratitude! Research shows that body appreciation is linked to higher levels of body satisfaction regardless of a person's weight, shape, and size (Homan et al., 2014).

While it may seem challenging at first, there's always something to be grateful for about your body, even if it's just one thing. Once you identify one aspect to appreciate, you'll likely discover more, leading to a growing list of loving thoughts about your body's strengths and capabilities. So, let's explore five simple yet effective body gratitude exercises to help you practice.

Body Scan With Gratitude

Sometimes, your body and mind can be out of sync. This disconnect can lead to stress and anxiety affecting your body without you fully realizing it (Scott, 2024). Body scan meditation helps you reconnect with your body by focusing on the present moment instead of worrying about the past or future. By becoming more attuned to your body, you can develop a greater sense of gratitude for its resilience and the ways it serves you each day.

Here's a step-by-step guide on how to perform a body scan focused on gratitude:

Begin by sitting or lying down in a quiet space where you won't be disturbed. Make sure you're comfortable and relaxed.

Close your eyes and focus inward.

Take a few deep breaths in through your nose and out through your mouth. This helps to center yourself and prepare for the practice.

Bring your attention to your feet. Notice any sensations, such as warmth, tingling, or heaviness.

Gradually move your focus up your body, part by part. Start with your legs, then move to your hips, torso, arms, and head.

As you scan each part of your body, pay attention to any sensations you feel, whether pleasant or unpleasant. Acknowledge these sensations without judgment. If you notice negative thoughts about your body, gently shift your focus back to gratitude.

For each body part, take a moment to express gratitude for what it does for you. For example, thank your legs for allowing you to walk or your heart for beating and circulating blood throughout your body.

Continue your scan slowly, taking deep breaths as you move up your body. Allow yourself to relax and release any tension you may find.

Once you've completed the scan, slowly open your eyes. Take a moment to reflect on the experience and how you feel.

Aim to practice this exercise regularly. By being consistent, you'll become more in tune with your body and grow a deeper appreciation for everything it does for you.

Thank-You Notes

By taking the time to express gratitude for different parts of your body, you can foster a positive and nurturing relationship with it. What simpler way to do that than by actually writing it a thank-you note?

Here's how it works:

Find a quiet place where you can reflect without interruptions. Think about different aspects of your body and how they contribute to your life.

Pick one or more body parts you want to express gratitude for. For example, you might choose your hands, heart, legs, or eyes for today.

Start writing a thank-you note to your chosen body parts. Be specific in your appreciation. For instance, thank your hands for helping you complete daily tasks, your heart for pumping blood and keeping you alive, or your legs for supporting you and allowing you to move around.

Write from the heart and be sincere in your gratitude. Focus on the positive aspects and the benefits each part of your body brings to your life.

Once you've written your thank-you notes, take a moment to read them over and reflect on the words. Notice how expressing gratitude for your body makes you feel.

This practice encourages you to acknowledge the ways your body supports you in your daily life. By writing thank-you notes addressed to your body, you strengthen your connection with it and enhance your appreciation for all the remarkable things it does for you.

Body Celebration Art

This exercise uses art as a way to express gratitude for your body. The goal is to celebrate the beauty and functionality of your body through creativity. There are many ways you can do this, but here is a simple guide to help get you started:

Choose your medium: Decide whether you want to draw, paint, or take photographs of your body. Choose a medium that you enjoy and feel comfortable with, or try something new that you've always wanted to explore!

Set an intention: Before you begin, set an intention to focus on the beauty and functionality of your body. This can shift your mindset away from negative thoughts about your appearance and allow you to focus on the amazing things your body does for you every day.

Select body parts to celebrate: Choose specific parts of your body to capture in your art. This could be anything from your hands and feet to your heart or eyes.

Create your art: Take your time to highlight the parts of your body you want to celebrate. Use different colors, shapes, and lines to express the qualities you admire. As you create, think about how your body helps you move through the world, accomplish tasks, and experience life. Let your art reflect the strength, resilience, and unique beauty your body offers. Don't be afraid to experiment and see where your creativity takes you!

Reflect on your creation: Once your art is complete, take a moment to reflect on it. Consider how it makes you feel about your body and the ways it has helped you shift your perspective toward appreciation.

If you feel comfortable, display your art in a place where you can see it regularly. This serves as a reminder of your body's beauty and the gratitude you hold for it.

Positive Mirror Reflection

This exercise involves standing in front of a mirror and focusing on different parts of your body, but, this time, instead of critiquing your appearance, you'll take the opportunity to express appreciation and gratitude for each part and acknowledge what it does for you.

Here's a step-by-step guide:

Choose a calm and quiet environment where you can stand in front of a full-length mirror without distractions.

Stand or sit comfortably in front of the mirror, and take a few deep breaths to relax.

Start by focusing on a specific part of your body. This could be your face, arms, legs, stomach, or any other area.

Instead of critiquing your body, express appreciation for the chosen body part. Acknowledge its functionality and the role it plays in your life. For example, thank your eyes for allowing you to see the world.

Use positive and kind language when expressing appreciation. Avoid any negative self-talk or comparisons.

After expressing gratitude for one part of your body, move on to another. Repeat the process, acknowledging each part's unique contributions and capabilities.

Once you've gone through each part of your body, take a moment to express appreciation for your body as a whole. Recognize the incredible ways your body supports you every day. For example, you could say, "Thank you, body, for carrying me through the world with strength every day."

Make this exercise a regular part of your routine. The more you practice, the more you'll experience a positive shift in your body image and self-esteem.

Morning Compliments

Starting your day with compliments for your body can set the tone for the entire day. This exercise helps you cultivate a mindset of gratitude and self-love by focusing on the strengths and beauty of your body rather than any perceived flaws.

Here's how you can practice morning compliments:

Pick a specific time each morning, such as right after waking up or during breakfast, to practice your morning compliments. This will help you establish a habit.

Choose a quiet, comfortable place where you can spend a few minutes alone, free from distractions.

Begin by speaking out loud compliments about your body. Focus on different parts, such as your skin, hair, eyes, legs, or arms, and express gratitude for each one.

Be specific about what you appreciate. For example, you could say, "I love how strong and capable my arms are," or "I'm grateful for my beautiful, expressive eyes."

After focusing on individual parts, take a moment to appreciate your body as a whole. Express gratitude for all that your body does for you and how it supports you every day.

Notice how you feel after expressing these compliments. You may find that you start your day with a more positive and confident outlook.

By incorporating morning compliments into your routine, you can build a stronger, more nurturing relationship with your body and start your day with a sense of gratitude and self-acceptance.

Finding Beauty in Imperfections

When you create something by hand, like painting a picture or making pottery, you often find the little imperfections charming and unique. Those quirks make the piece special and personal. But when it comes to our bodies, we don't always offer ourselves the same grace. Instead, we're quick to criticize small flaws.

Imagine if you treated your body with the same acceptance you have for your creations. See your freckles as beautiful brushstrokes on a canvas, your laugh lines as marks of countless moments of joy, and your stretch marks as proof of growth and change. Shifting your perspective can be challenging, especially in a world that often promotes a narrow view of beauty. However, what's important is to keep trying.

With that in mind, here are some tips to help you appreciate the uniqueness of every body and discover the beauty in imperfections:

View your body's markings as badges of experience: Treat your scars, stretch marks, and laugh lines as symbols of your journey through life. They represent growth, exploration, and cherished memories.Additionally, consider your body's changes as evidence of the milestones you've reached and challenges you've overcome. Celebrate them as proof of a life lived fully.

Celebrate differences: Instead of comparing yourself to others, embrace your uniqueness and individual beauty. Celebrate the features that set you apart and recognize that what you perceive as imperfections may be the very aspects of yourself that make you special and memorable.

Notice how you find beauty in others, especially those who don't conform to traditional beauty standards: Pay attention to how you admire their confidence, charm, and grace, even if they have features that society might label as "imperfect." Observe how their individuality sets them apart and makes them captivating to you. By seeing beauty in others, you open yourself up to seeing your own body in a different light.

Practice acceptance over control: It's natural to want to change certain aspects of your body. However, learning to accept your body as it is can be much more fulfilling. Acknowledge the aspects of your body that you cannot change, whether it's your height, your natural body shape, or features you were born with. Rather than trying to control or alter these aspects, focus on embracing them as part of your unique identity. Letting go of the need to control or change what you cannot opens you up to a new kind of freedom.

Seek out stories and art that embrace imperfections: One of the most impactful ways to change your perspective on beauty is by surrounding yourself with stories and art that celebrate unique and imperfect beauty. When you engage with books, films, photography, and other artistic mediums that showcase a diverse range of bodies and perspectives, you expose yourself to different ways of seeing the world and beauty. This exposure can challenge the traditional, narrow standards of beauty that are often perpetuated in mainstream media.

Get in touch with nature: Nature's beauty is often found in its raw, unpolished imperfections. Spend time outdoors and take in the natural world around you. Notice the unique textures of trees, the diverse colors and shapes of leaves, or the variety of patterns on butterfly wings. Reflect on how these imperfections make nature extraordinary and inspiring. Applying this mindset to your own body can help you find beauty in your imperfections, recognizing them as part of your own unique natural wonder.

With consistent practice and mindfulness, you can begin to appreciate your body's uniqueness and see it as it truly is: a living, breathing work of perfectly imperfect art!

***

Now that you've learned how to prioritize function over aesthetics, celebrate imperfections, and cultivate gratitude for your body, let's look ahead. In the next chapter, we'll discuss how you can fully embrace a body-positive lifestyle that empowers you to thrive! It's time to explore how to create a future where you consistently love and honor yourself for who you are.

Establishing a Body Positive Future

You are not a mistake. You are not a problem to be solved. But you won't discover this until you are willing to stop banging your head against the wall of shaming and caging and fearing yourself. -Geneen Roth

Imagine waking up in the morning, feeling truly at ease in your own skin. You start the day with a quick stretch, realizing you can now touch your toes without any strain—something you couldn't do a few months back. You smile at your newfound flexibility, feeling strong and ready to take on the day.

After your stretch, you head into the kitchen. You think about what you feel like eating and decide on an English breakfast, a meal you learned to prepare during a trip to the UK a month ago. You savor every bite, knowing you've been craving this meal since your travels.

You follow up breakfast with a blueberry muffin and a cup of coffee. A quiet voice in the back of your mind questions whether you're eating too much, especially since you had a bowl of ice cream the night before. You take three slow, deep breaths to calm any doubts, then affirm your choice by giving yourself permission to enjoy eating. You're glad you did because the muffin tastes amazing!

After breakfast, you take a quick shower and put on clothes you picked out the night before—a summer dress you might not have worn in the past because you thought it revealed too much of your arms. Now, you smile at your reflection in the mirror, appreciating how the dress showcases your style and makes you feel confident and pretty.

Work is hectic, but you tackle your tasks with energy and focus. When your stomach growls at lunchtime, you take a break to eat a delicious meal with coworkers and clear your mind with a short walk. This break re-energizes you, helping you see creative solutions to your tasks and boosting your productivity.

After work, you enjoy dinner at home, then unwind with a bath, meditation, and reading. You watch an episode of a favorite show before heading to bed at your usual time to ensure you get enough sleep for the next day.

How did this visualization make you feel?

Everyone's circumstances and journey are different, but this is one simple glimpse into what a sustainable, body-positive lifestyle might look like. As you can see, the focus is on nurturing your overall well-being and fully experiencing life, rather than fixating on restrictions or appearances. Sure, moments of doubt might still pop up from time to time. But the good news is, you now have the tools to conquer them and trust your own instincts!

Cultivating Body Image Resilience

Resilience is the ability to adapt and recover quickly when faced with challenges or setbacks. Essentially, it's about bouncing back stronger from life's curveballs. When you're resilient, you can maintain or swiftly regain your mental and emotional balance even in tough situations. Resilient people handle stress, trauma, and big life changes with grace, learning and growing from every experience.

But, did you know there is also such a thing as body image resilience? It refers to the ability to navigate and bounce back from challenges related to how you perceive your body. It involves managing negative thoughts and feelings about your appearance while being open to growth and learning from these experiences. People with body image resilience can adapt to societal pressures, media influences, and personal setbacks related to body image while still maintaining a positive relationship with their bodies.

Body image resilience emerged from the work of Lexie Kite, who developed the theory by combining self-objectification theory with resilience theory. The idea is that people can become stronger because of the body struggles they experience rather than despite it. In other words, instead of allowing the pain and challenges related to body image to break you, you can use these experiences as opportunities for learning and growth (Duncan, 2018). This is precisely what we are aiming to achieve, as we cannot fully escape external influences and harmful messaging. However, we can control how we respond to them and choose to no longer buy into toxic ideas and behaviors.

Building body image resilience is similar to strengthening your mental and emotional resilience. Let's talk about how to take steps toward it.

Find a Sense of Purpose

Having a purpose can help you develop resilience by providing you with a clear sense of direction and a reason to keep pushing forward, even during tough times. When you know what drives you, there are no failures—only obstacles to overcome and learn from. Instead of getting bogged down by setbacks, you can focus on your larger goals and keep your eyes on the prize.

Similar to success, defining purpose is subjective and can vary from person to person. Psychologists acknowledge two main types of purpose. The first involves setting specific life goals that guide your actions and decisions. For instance, you might discover that your purpose is to advocate for the environment or become a doctor to help the sick.

However, not everyone has an overarching life goal, and that's totally fine too. The second type involves feeling a sense of purpose even without tying it to a specific goal. This kind of purpose means you wake up in the morning feeling motivated by simple reasons like planning a trip or just feeling generally excited to tackle your tasks for the day.

Whichever type of purpose you have, research shows that it can positively impact your health and well-being. A sense of purpose can help you live longer, manage stress more effectively, make healthier choices, and maintain better brain function (Hirsch, 2024).

Finding a sense of purpose can take time, but here are some tips to get you started:

Reflect on what matters to you: Take some time to think about your values, passions, and the causes that you care about. Consider how these might guide your direction and actions. Here are some prompts to guide you on your reflection:

Write about the activities, experiences, or people that bring you the most happiness and fulfillment. How can you incorporate more of these into your life?

Consider the topics or causes that ignite your enthusiasm. How can you pursue these passions more fully?

List the values that resonate most with you, such as honesty, compassion, or creativity. How do these values influence your decisions and actions?

Reflect on past obstacles and how you handled them. What did you learn from these experiences?

Think about how you want to be remembered. What impact do you want to make on the world?

Explore new interests: Trying new activities and hobbies can help you discover what you enjoy and may lead you to uncover new passions.

Connect with others: Surround yourself with people who share your interests and values. These connections can provide inspiration and support as you pursue your purpose.

Give back: Volunteering or helping others can be a meaningful way to contribute to your community and find purpose in your actions.

Your sense of purpose may evolve over time as you grow and learn more about yourself. So, remember to keep an open mind and be patient with yourself.

Build a Strong Social Support Network

Building a strong support network is like having a personal cheer squad that keeps you grounded and empowered. Friends, family, and mentors can offer a listening ear, share helpful advice, and lift your spirits when times get tough. This reliable team can provide both emotional encouragement and practical help, allowing you to navigate life's obstacles with greater resilience. In fact, research shows that having strong social support can improve health and wellness, while poor social support has been linked to depression, loneliness, and increased risks of alcohol use, cardiovascular disease, and suicide (Cherry, 2023).

Here are some strategies for building and sustaining meaningful social support:

Nurture existing relationships: Regularly keep in touch with friends and family, whether through phone calls, texts, or in-person visits. Share your experiences openly and listen to theirs, as this mutual exchange strengthens your connections and builds trust. Make time for quality conversations and plan activities together to create meaningful memories.

Join interest-based groups: Engage with people who share your hobbies or passions. Whether it's a book club, sports team, crafting circle, or gardening group, these communities allow you to connect with others who have similar interests. This shared enthusiasm can be a great conversation starter and a way to form lasting friendships.

Volunteer in your community: Volunteering allows you to contribute to a cause and connect with like-minded people. Look for opportunities that align with your interests, whether that's helping at a local shelter, participating in a community cleanup, or assisting with an event. Not only will you be making a positive impact, but you'll also enrich your social support network.

Communicate openly: Share your thoughts and feelings with people you trust. Honest and open communication allows others to understand you better and fosters deeper, more meaningful relationships. Remember that listening is also a key part of communication, so be present and attentive when others share their perspectives with you.

Offer support to others: Providing help and encouragement to others builds mutual trust and deepens relationships. Don't be afraid to show others that you care!

Respect boundaries: Establish healthy boundaries in your relationships to ensure they remain balanced and mutually supportive. Setting clear limits on your time, energy, and emotional investment helps you maintain your well-being while also showing respect for others.

Participate in local events: Attend community gatherings, festivals, and social activities to meet new people and strengthen your bonds with those you already know. These events provide opportunities to connect over shared interests and create a sense of belonging within your local community.

Remember that relationships are a two-way street, so respect other people's boundaries and be ready to communicate and support them, too. Additionally, don't be afraid to seek professional help if needed. A therapist or counselor can guide you in navigating and strengthening your connections with others. They can also provide support for mental health concerns and equip you with the tools to manage stress, anxiety, or depression that might otherwise strain relationships.

Learn to Accept Change

By accepting change as a natural part of life and staying adaptable, you can handle challenges with ease and even turn them into opportunities for growth. While others may struggle with sudden changes, resilient people welcome them as a chance to explore new directions and expand their horizons. This doesn't mean they don't find it difficult, but they face it head-on anyway. This flexibility not only helps you bounce back from setbacks but also empowers you to thrive in any situation.

Here are some ways you can become more flexible and adaptable:

Cultivate a growth mindset: Instead of seeing setbacks as failures, treat them as chances to learn and improve. For example, if you face a challenge at work, reflect on what you can do differently next time rather than dwelling on the mistake.

Practice mindfulness: Being present in the moment allows you to respond to situations thoughtfully. Try meditation or deep-breathing exercises to help you stay calm and focused in the face of change.

Stay organized and plan ahead: Having a plan or routine can provide a solid foundation for adaptability. For example, keeping a daily to-do list helps you stay on track while being ready to shift priorities if needed.

Develop problem-solving skills: Practice analyzing situations and coming up with creative solutions. For example, if your work project hits a roadblock, brainstorm different ways to approach the issue.

Embrace uncertainty: Life is full of unknowns, so learning to accept uncertainty can help you adapt when things change unexpectedly. Instead of fearing your next step, focus on the possibilities it may bring.

Set realistic expectations: Understand that life is unpredictable, and things may not always go according to plan. For instance, if a trip gets canceled, focus on what you can do instead of dwelling on the disappointment.

Learn to let go: Holding on to old habits or expectations can hinder your ability to adapt. If your old morning routine no longer works for you, try a new one!

The secret to accepting the inevitability of change is to stay open-minded. Embrace new ideas, perspectives, and experiences. Train your mind to view challenges as opportunities to learn and grow.

Set Goals

Setting goals helps develop resilience by giving you a clear sense of direction, which can keep you motivated during challenging times. When you have specific objectives in mind, you are more likely to stay focused and push through adversity. Goals also provide a measure of progress, allowing you to see how far you've come and adjust your approach as needed. This flexibility helps you adapt to changing circumstances and overcome obstacles. Additionally, achieving smaller milestones along the way can boost your confidence, ultimately contributing to your overall resilience.

Here are some tips to guide you in setting achievable goals:

Be specific: Clearly define what you want to achieve. Instead of setting a vague goal like "learn a new language," specify exactly what you want to accomplish, such as "hold a 15-minute conversation in Spanish within six months."

Make goals measurable: Establish concrete criteria to measure your progress. For example, if your goal is to improve your writing, set a target of writing 500 words a day.

Set realistic goals: Aim for goals that are challenging but attainable given your current circumstances and resources. For example, instead of setting a goal to read 20 books in one month, aim for a more achievable goal like reading one or two books a month, depending on your schedule. Overly ambitious goals can lead to frustration and burnout.

Break down big goals: Divide larger goals into smaller, manageable tasks. For instance, instead of being overwhelmed by a goal like "write a novel," break it down into smaller tasks such as outlining the plot, creating character profiles, and writing a set number of pages each day. This approach makes the goal more manageable and gives you the chance to celebrate progress as you complete each step.

Set a timeframe: Establish a deadline or timeframe for your goals. For example, if your goal is to learn a new language, set a deadline to complete a language course in six months. This timeframe helps you stay focused and consistent with your practice, ensuring you make steady progress toward your goal (Lindberg, 2020).

Be open to adjusting your goals as needed. Remember that life circumstances can change, and flexibility allows you to pivot without losing sight of your overall vision.

How to Set Body-Positive Goals

While we're on the topic of goal-setting, creating ones specifically related to your body image can help you sustain progress and thrive. Now that you have a solid foundation for setting achievable goals, let's create some long-term, body-positive ones!

Here's a simple guide on how:

Focus on growth: Shift your mindset from aiming for weight loss to prioritizing personal growth. This could include goals like increasing your strength, improving your flexibility, or enhancing your overall fitness level. Be honest with yourself and make sure you're not unconsciously using these reasons as an excuse to lose weight.

Emphasize what you can do: Celebrate your body's capabilities instead of fixating on insecurities. Set goals based on what your body can accomplish, such as running a certain distance or mastering a new yoga pose.

Make them process-oriented: Focus on the actions and habits that will lead you toward your desired outcomes, rather than fixating on specific end results. For example, you can aim to meditate for five minutes each morning or commit to trying a new physical activity every week.

Be kind to yourself: Avoid goals that reinforce negative thoughts about your body. Instead, set goals that encourage self-care and self-compassion, like taking time to relax or eating nourishing foods.

Listen to your body: Tune in to what your body is telling you and align your goals accordingly—whether it needs more rest, different types of exercise, or a change in routine. For example, if you're feeling tired, consider swapping a high-intensity workout for a yoga session or taking a rest day. This way, you stay connected with your body and avoid unnecessary strain.

Incorporate rest and recovery: Prioritize rest and recovery as part of your goals. Adequate sleep, relaxation, and self-care are essential for overall well-being and can help you stay motivated.

Choose inclusive activities: Participate in physical activities or hobbies that are inclusive and welcoming to all body types. Join dance classes or sports clubs that emphasize enjoyment and self-expression rather than competition. This type of activity can help you connect with your body in a fun, supportive environment and appreciate the different shapes and sizes that people come in.

Set boundaries: Learn to say no to activities or experiences that don't align with your body-positive goals. For example, if a fitness class emphasizes weight loss over enjoyment, you might opt out and instead find an inclusive class that values health and self-care. Always prioritize your well-being by respecting your boundaries.

Remember that creating a body-positive lifestyle is a process, and getting used to new habits takes time. Periodically reflect on your progress and reassess your goals to help you stay on track and make adjustments as needed.

Additionally, surround yourself with body-positive role models and relationships; their outlook can inspire and reinforce your goals. They can also remind you that a healthy, body-positive life is possible and that you are not alone in striving for one.

Conclusion

Beauty is narrowly defined by society, emphasizing physical appearance and youthfulness above all else. When we cannot meet these standards, it often leads to a damaged body image. However, true beauty goes beyond what the eyes can see; it is deeply intertwined with confidence and a genuine appreciation for oneself. When we embrace ourselves for who we are, we not only begin healing our relationship with our bodies, but we also radiate an inner glow that cannot be achieved through external means.

As you turn the final pages of this book, remember to apply what you've learned from the S.P.A.R.K.L.E. framework. **S**tart by understanding the complexities of body image and equipping yourself with knowledge. Then, **p**ave the road to self-compassion by treating yourself with kindness and respect. Next, **a**ccept body positivity by celebrating diverse body types, including your own. Don't forget to **r**ewrite the narrative by challenging negative self-talk and replacing it with affirmations and encouragement. Afterward, **k**now how to care for your body by listening to its needs and prioritizing self-care. **L**ean on function rather than aesthetics. And, last but not least, **e**stablish a body-positive future by cultivating resilience and setting achievable goals rooted in self-love and acceptance.

By embracing this framework, you pave the way for a more meaningful and genuine life where empowerment and confidence thrive. As astronomer, naturalist, educator, and all-around amazing woman Maria Mitchell once said, "There is no cosmetic for beauty like happiness" (Mitchell, n.d.).

It's time for you to find happiness in your own body and truly S.P.A.R.K.L.E. from within!

***

Did you enjoy *Mind Over Mirror* and find it insightful? How did you connect with the guidance and stories in the book? Let us know what resonated most with you or tell us about your body image journey. Your feedback can help others on a similar path discover the book and inspire them on their journey to self-acceptance and empowerment. Thank you for being part of this important conversation!

References

Abbott, B. (2012, February 14). Teaching girls to prioritise function over form for better body image. *The Conversation.* https://theconversation.com/teaching-girls-to-prioritise-function-over-form-for-better-body-image-11620

Abrams, Z. (2022, March 1). The burden of weight stigma. *American Psychological Association.* https://www.apa.org/monitor/2022/03/news-weight-stigma

Alleva, J. (2021, November 22). *Why body-positive social media may be good for you.* Psychology Today. https://www.psychologytoday.com/intl/blog/mind-your-body/202111/why-body-positive-social-media-may-be-good-you

American Heart Association. (2021, March 16). *How much physical activity do you need?* https://www.heart.org/en/healthy-living/fitness/fitness-basics/aha-recs-for-physical-activity-infographic

Ankrom, S. (2024, February 16). *Need a breather? Try these 9 breathing exercises to relieve anxiety.* Verywell Mind. https://www.verywellmind.com/abdominal-breathing-2584115

Anti-Bullying Alliance. (n.d.). *Appearance-targeted bullying.* https://anti-bullyingalliance.org.uk/tools-information/all-about-bull ying/at-risk-groups/appearance-targeted-bullying

Ayuda, T. (2021, October 16). *Postpartum snapback culture hurt my mental health. Here's how I made fitness my own again.* SELF. https://www.self.com/story/postpartum-snapback-culture-fitness

Benner, C. (2022, October 26). *Why is self-compassion so hard for some people?* Greater Good. https://greatergood.berkeley.edu/article/item/why_is_self_compassio n_so_hard_for_some_people

Bjarnadottir, A. (2023, April 11). *Do detox diets and cleanses really work?* Healthline. https://www.healthline.com/nutrition/detox-diets-101

Borges, A., & Ryu, J. (2023, August 7). *15 of the best journaling apps to make self-reflection more convenient.* SELF. https://www.self.com/story/best-journal-apps

Bredehoft, D. (2023, August 7). *The science behind self-affirmations.* Psychology Today. https://www.psychologytoday.com/intl/blog/the-age-of-overindulgen ce/202307/the-science-behind-self-affirmations

Bronner, S. (2015, June 18). Serena Williams: "I had to come to terms with loving myself." *HuffPost.* https://www.huffpost.com/entry/serena-williams-body-image_n_7 599214

Brooks, D. (2021, June 24). Why is it ok to be mean to the ugly? *The New York Times.* https://www.nytimes.com/2021/06/24/opinion/why-is-it-ok-to-be-mean-to-the-ugly.html

Cherry, K. (2023, March 3). *How social support contributes to psychological health.* Verywell Mind.

https://www.verywellmind.com/social-support-for-psychological-health-4119970

Coelho, P. (2013). *Manuscript Found in Accra*. Alfred A. Knopf.

Collins, D. (2022, April 20). *The importance of a healthy body image: 4 ways to improve yours*. One Medical. https://www.onemedical.com/blog/healthy-living/importance-healthy-body-image-4-ways-improve-yours/

Connor, E. (2023, June 22). *What are freckles, why do they appear, and more*. Healthline. https://www.healthline.com/health/what-are-freckles

Crosta, P. (2023, November 13). Everything you need to know about cellulite. *Medical News Today*. https://www.medicalnewstoday.com/articles/149465

Dailymail.com Reporter. (2015, July 15). "A group of girls jumped me at school": Model Winnie Harlow recalls years of bullying and abuse in powerful new essay about her skin condition. *MailOnline*. https://www.dailymail.co.uk/femail/article-3162357/Model-Winnie-Harlow-recalls-years-bullying-abuse-powerful-new-essay-skin-condition.html

Daw, M. (2021, May 3). *Bravely being me-my body image story*. Brave Heart Wellbeing. https://braveheartwellbeing.com.au/body-image/bravely-being-me-my-body-image-story/

Deschene, L. (n.d.). *Lori Deschene quotes*. Goodreads. https://www.goodreads.com/quotes/6527635-we-can-t-hate-ourselves-into-a-version-of-ourselves-we

DoSomething.org. (n.d.). *11 facts about body image*. Retrieved March 25, 2024, from https://www.dosomething.org/us/facts/11-facts-about-body-image

Duncan, K. (2018, March 30). What is body image resiliency? *Carolina News and Reporter.* https://carolinanewsandreporter.cic.sc.edu/what-is-body-image-resiliency/

Fleps, B. (2021, April 21). *Social media effects on body image and eating disorders.* Illinois State University. https://news.illinoisstate.edu/2021/04/social-media-effects-on-body-image-and-eating-disorders/

Fletcher, J. (2021, January 28). When and how to spend a rest day. *Medical News Today.* https://www.medicalnewstoday.com/articles/rest-day

Fredrek, C. (2017, September 25). *The truth about body image during midlife: Feel beautiful, glowing, and empowered.* Healing Matters. https://healingmatters.ca/truth-body-image-midlife-feel-beautiful-glowing-empowered/

Fuller, K. (2022a, June 28). *Difference between disordered eating and eating disorders.* Verywell Mind. https://www.verywellmind.com/difference-between-disordered-eating-and-eating-disorders-5184548

Fuller, K. (2022b, June 30). *Body positivity vs. body neutrality.* Verywell Mind. https://www.verywellmind.com/body-positivity-vs-body-neutrality-5184565

Glowiak, M. (2024, January 23). *What is self-care and why is it important for you?* Southern New Hampshire University. https://www.snhu.edu/about-us/newsroom/health/what-is-self-care

Gourlay, C. (2020, April 30). *Self-compassion, not self-indulgence – Looking after number one.* Caroline Gourlay Business Psychology. https://www.carolinegourlay.co.uk/looking-after-number-one/

Greenberg, M. (2015, December 6). *The 3 most common causes of insecurity and how to beat them.* Psychology Today. https://www.psychologytoday.com/us/blog/the-mindful-self-exp ress/201512/the-3-most-common-causes-insecurity-and-how-bea t-them

Gruys, K. (2019, May 1). How does appearance affect our success? *Nevada   Today.* https://www.unr.edu/nevada-today/news/2019/atp-appearance-success

Guillaume, J. (2015, February 28). 9 stories of women's complicated relationships   with   their   bodies. *BuzzFeed.* https://www.buzzfeed.com/jennaguillaume/stories-of-womens-b ody-image-struggle

Gutman-Wei, R. (2023, September 7). We have no drugs to treat the deadliest   eating   disorder. *The   Atlantic.* https://www.theatlantic.com/health/archive/2023/09/anorexia-d rug-resistance-eating-disorder/675246/

Harvard Health. (2019, June 24). *Why people become overweight.* https://www.health.harvard.edu/staying-healthy/why-people-be come-overweight

Haupt, A. (2023, July 17). *7 tips for showing yourself some self-compassion.*   Everyday   Health. https://www.everydayhealth.com/emotional-health/tips-for-sho wing-yourself-some-self-compassion/

Hayes, L. (n.d.). *Lisa M. Hayes quotes.* Goodreads. https://www.goodreads.com/quotes/655867-be-careful-how-you -are-talking-to-yourself-because-you

Hirsch, M. (2024, April 1). *All about purpose: What it means and why it's   so   good   for   you.* Everyday   Health. https://www.everydayhealth.com/emotional-health/all-about-havin

g-a-sense-of-purpose-what-it-means-and-why-its-so-good-for-you/

Homan, K., Sedlak, B., & Boyd, E. (2014). Gratitude buffers the adverse effect of viewing the thin ideal on body dissatisfaction. *Body Image, 11*(3), 245-250. https://doi.org/10.1016/j.bodyim.2014.03.005

How to deal with and overcome body insecurity. (2024, January 31). W   i   t   h   i   n   . https://withinhealth.com/learn/articles/understanding-body-insecurity

Hungate, R. (2021, November 23). *Misconceptions about what you might think is healthy eating.* Eating Disorder Hope. https://www.eatingdisorderhope.com/nutrition-counseling-eating-disorders/misconceptions-healthy-eating

Illinois Department of Public Health. (n.d.). *Facts about women's wellness-exercise.* Retrieved April 10, 2024, from http://www.idph.state.il.us/about/womenshealth/factsheets/exer.htm

Johnson, J. (2018, September 5). How to tell if stress is affecting your sleep. *Medical News Today.* https://www.medicalnewstoday.com/articles/322994

Johnson, M. (2022, February 11). *The 4 components of body image.* Psychology   Today. https://www.psychologytoday.com/us/blog/the-savvy-psychologist/202202/the-4-components-body-image

Kay, K. (2012, June 10). Elderly struck by "epidemic" of body image and eating disorders. *The Guardian.* https://www.theguardian.com/society/2012/jun/10/body-image-elderly-hidden-illness

Keltner, D. (2012, July 31). *The compassionate species.* Greater Good. https://greatergood.berkeley.edu/article/item/the_compassionate_ species

Kite, L., & Kite, L. (2016, April 26). *From body anxiety to body image activism: Our   story.*   More   than   a   Body. https://www.morethanabody.org/body-anxiety-to-body-image-ac tivism/

Kuppersmith, N., & Kennedy, C. (2005). *Perils of skipping meals.* University   of   Louisville. https://louisville.edu/medicine/departments/familymedicine/files /L081611.pdf

Large,   C.   (2022,   January   29).   *My "body   positivity"   story.*   The   Wild   Woman. https://thewildwoman.blog/2022/01/29/my-body-positivity-story/

Lawler, M. (2022, February 2). *All about body image: How psychologists define it and how it affects health and well-being.* Everyday Health. https://www.everydayhealth.com/body-image/

Leech, J. (2024, January 6). *9 reasons you don't need to fear healthy carbs.*   Healthline. https://www.healthline.com/nutrition/9-reasons-not-to-fear-car bs

Lees, E. (2020, April 15). *How can the clothes we buy impact our confidence?*   Happiful. https://happiful.com/how-can-the-clothes-we-buy-impact-our-c onfidence

Lindberg, S. (2020, November 26). *Tips for goal setting.* Verywell M   i   n   d   . https://www.verywellmind.com/tips-for-goal-setting-self-impro vement-4688587

Lindner, J. (2023, December 20). *The most surprising beauty standards statistics in 2024*. Gitnux. https://gitnux.org/beauty-standards-statistics/

Mendell, J. (2015, April 11). How refusing to diet and starting to live my life helped me lose 40 pounds. *Women's Health*. https://www.womenshealthmag.com/weight-loss/a19912428/jamie-mendell-wl-success-story/

Mental Health First Aid USA. (2021, July 27). *How breathing can help reduce stress*. https://www.mentalhealthfirstaid.org/2021/07/how-breathing-can-help-reduce-stress/

Mental Health Foundation. (n.d.-a). *Body image in childhood*. https://www.mentalhealth.org.uk/explore-mental-health/articles/body-image-report-executive-summary/body-image-childhood

Mental Health Foundation. (n.d.-b). *Body image in later life*. https://www.mentalhealth.org.uk/our-work/research/body-image-how-we-think-and-feel-about-our-bodies/body-image-later-life

Mitchell, M. (n.d.). *Maria Mitchell quotes*. Goodreads. https://www.goodreads.com/quotes/549613-there-is-no-cosmetic-for-beauty-like-happiness

National Eating Disorders Collaboration. (n.d.). *Body image*. Retrieved March 26, 2024, from https://nedc.com.au/eating-disorders/eating-disorders-explained/body-image

Neff, K. (2003). Self-compassion: An alternative conceptualization of a healthy attitude toward oneself. *Self and Identity, 2*, 85-101. https://doi.org/10.1080/15298860390129863

Ngo, N. (2019). What historical ideals of women's shapes teach us about women's self-perception and body decisions today. *AMA Journal of Ethics, 21*(10), 879-901. https://doi.org/10.1001/amajethics.2019.879.

Nunez, K. (2020a, August 10). *The benefits of Progressive Muscle Relaxation and how to do it.* Healthline. https://www.healthline.com/health/progressive-muscle-relaxation

Nunez, K. (2020b, September 10). *The benefits of guided imagery and how to do it.* Healthline. https://www.healthline.com/health/guided-imagery

Pacanowski, C., Linde, J., & Neumark-Sztainer, D. (2016). Self-weighing: Helpful or harmful for psychological well-being? A review of the literature. *Current Obesity Reports, 4*(1), 65-72. https://doi.org/10.1007/s13679-015-0142-2

Pemberton, M. (2020, February 18). 27 Amazing things your body does. *Reader's Digest.* https://www.readersdigest.co.uk/health/medical-myths/27-amazing-things-your-body-does

Petre, A. (2022, May 18). *6 common types of eating disorders (and their symptoms).* Healthline. https://www.healthline.com/nutrition/common-eating-disorder

Pratik. (2022, March 31). *Relationship between fashion and body positivity clothing in 2022.* IIAD. https://www.iiad.edu.in/the-circle/fashion-and-body-positivity/

Puhl, R. (2021, June 12). Weight stigma study in the U.S. and 5 other nations shows the worldwide problem of such prejudice. *Washington Post.* https://www.washingtonpost.com/health/overweight-discrimination-common-harmful/2021/06/11/2946c538-c88c-11eb-afd0-9726f7ecoba6_story.html

Putham, L. (2015, March 4). "Hot convict" Jeremy Meeks to begin modeling after prison. *New York Post.* https://nypost.com/2015/03/04/hot-convict-jeremy-meeks-to-begin-modeling-after-prison/

Raypole, C. (2020, September 1). *Positive affirmations: Too good to be true?* Healthline. https://www.healthline.com/health/mental-health/do-affirmations-work

Reid, L. (2020, September 4). *Interest in body positivity and self-care thriving in 2020.* Brandwatch. https://www.brandwatch.com/blog/react-body-positivity-self-care-thriving/

Richards, L. (2022, March 18). What is positive self-talk? *Medical News Today.* https://www.medicalnewstoday.com/articles/positive-self-talk

Roth, G. (n.d.). *Geneen Roth quotes.* AZ Quotes. https://www.azquotes.com/quote/805934

Roth, G. (2010). *Women, Food and God: An Unexpected Path to Almost Everything.* Scribner.

Ruggeri, A. (2022, October 17). Bounce-back culture: Why new mums are expected to "snap back." *BBC.* https://www.bbc.com/worklife/article/20221017-bounce-back-culture-how-pressure-to-snapback-hurts-new-mothers

Salzberg, S. (2017). *Real Love: The Art of Mindful Connection.* Flatiron Books.

Scott, E. (2023, November 22). *The toxic effects of negative self-talk.* Verywell Mind. https://www.verywellmind.com/negative-self-talk-and-how-it-affects-us-4161304

Scott, E. (2024, February 12). *What is body scan meditation?* Verywell M i n d . https://www.verywellmind.com/body-scan-meditation-why-and-how-3144782

Shapiro, B. (2018, September 11). Beauty is more diverse than ever. But is it diverse enough? *The New York Times.* https://www.nytimes.com/2018/09/11/style/beauty-diversity.html

Siddhanti, P. (2021, March 8). *The body positivity project: Stories from real women.* My Swiss Story. https://myswissstory.com/the-body-positivity-project-stories-from-real-women/

Sidibe, G. (n.d.). *Gabourey Sidibe quotes.* Goodreads. https://www.goodreads.com/quotes/8797587-one-day-i-decided-that-i-was-beautiful-and-so

SingleCare Team. (2024, January 24). *Stress statistics 2024: How common is stress and who's most affected?* The Checkup. https://www.singlecare.com/blog/news/stress-statistics/

Stanborough, R. (2020, November 25). *What to know about a negative body image and how to overcome it.* Healthline. https://www.healthline.com/health/negative-body-image

Stone, E. (n.d.). *Emma Stone quotes.* Quotefancy. https://quotefancy.com/quote/1431678/Emma-Stone-I-can-t-think-of-any-better-representation-of-beauty-than-someone-who-is

Sutton, J. (2018, May 14). *5 benefits of journaling for mental health.* PositivePsychology.com. https://positivepsychology.com/benefits-of-journaling/

Tee-Melegrito, R. (2023, March 28). What are examples of self-care? *Medical News Today.* https://www.medicalnewstoday.com/articles/self-care-examples

The Drew Barrymore Show. (2020). *Winnie Harlow credits her family for normalizing her vitiligo | Wildflower* [Video]. YouTube. https://www.youtube.com/watch?v=RtQfPPHTPXU

The Healthline Editorial Team. (2018, January 20). *Bones of foot.* Healthline. https://www.healthline.com/human-body-maps/bones-of-foot

The importance of good nutrition. (2023, October 10). Tufts Health P l a n . https://www.tuftsmedicarepreferred.org/healthy-living/importa nce-good-nutrition

University of North Carolina at Chapel Hill. (2008, April 23). Three out of four American women have disordered eating, survey suggests. *ScienceDaily.* https://www.sciencedaily.com/releases/2008/04/080422202514.ht m

Van Edwards, V. (2016, May 10). *Beauty standards: See how body types change through history.* Science of People. https://www.scienceofpeople.com/beauty-standards/

Voges, M., Giabbiconi, C.-M., Schone, B., Waldorf, M., Hartmann, A., & Vocks, S. (2019). Gender differences in body evaluation: Do men show more self-serving double standards than women? *Frontiers in Psychology, 10.* https://doi.org/10.3389/fpsyg.2019.00544

Waheed, N. (n.d.). *Nayyirah Waheed quotes.* Goodreads. https://www.goodreads.com/quotes/7685383-and-i-said-to-my-b ody-softly-i-want-to

Want to exercise more? You're much more likely to stick with an activity you enjoy. (2017, January 15). The Muscle Clinic. https://www.muscleclinic.co.uk/want-exercise-youre-much-likel y-stick-activity-enjoy/

Watson, E. (n.d.). *Emma Watson quotes*. Goodreads. https://www.goodreads.com/quotes/7680994-feeling-beautiful-has-nothing-to-do-with-what-you-look

World Health Organization. (2020, April 29). *Healthy diet.* https://www.who.int/news-room/fact-sheets/detail/healthy-diet